100 GREATS

CUMBERLAND
RUGBY LEAGUE

Cumbrian Delight. The greatest of all Cumbrian administrators, Tom Mitchell holds the Lancashire Cup after Workington Town's historic 16-13 victory over Wigan at Warrington in 1977. Three Cumbrian greats, skipper Paul Charlton, Arnie Walker and Peter Gorley share Tom's rapture.

100 GREATS

CUMBERLAND
RUGBY LEAGUE

COMPILED BY
ROBERT GATE

TEMPUS

The target for all aspiring Cumbrian Rugby League players – a county cap. This one belonged to Maryport-born Billy Dixon, who won fame as a utility back with Oldham.

Front cover picture: Ike Southward
Back cover pictures (from top to bottom): Martin Hodgson, Billy Little and Jim Brough

First published 2002

Tempus Publishing Limited
The Mill, Brimscombe Port,
Stroud, Gloucestershire, GL5 2QG

© Robert Gate, 2002

The right of Robert Gate to be identified as the Author
of this work has been asserted by him in accordance with the
Copyrights, Designs and Patents Act 1988.

British Library Cataloguing in Publication Data.
A catalogue record for this book is available from the British Library.

ISBN 0 7524 2731 8

Typesetting and origination by Tempus Publishing Limited
Printed in Great Britain by Midway Colour Print, Wiltshire

Introduction

There are apparently more people named Gate in Cumbria than anywhere else on Earth. So far, however, no evidence has been produced to prove that any of my family came from the region, although if I were to turn into a genealogist it is pretty certain that there would be some Cumbrian skeletons in my cupboard.

It has always irked me that no one has ever set down in written form the great debt which Rugby League owes to the clubs of the old Cumberland and Westmoreland counties. The southern clubs of Lancashire and Yorkshire have been pillaging the North-West for its rugby talent since before the Northern Union was founded in 1895, but there were always plenty of good young players to take the place of those who left.

I first had the idea of compiling a book on the outstanding players of Cumberland in about 1996. I was on a mission to watch Halifax play a night game at Workington with my good friend Henry Skrzypecki, an architect with a passion for surveying Rugby League and soccer grounds. Part of the day was set aside for Henry to call in at Whitehaven to reconnoitre the Recreation Ground. As we drove up the scenic coastal route, I got to thinking of all the great Cumbrian players who had graced the game down the years and thought there must be a book in it somewhere.

The thought was reinforced by my wife, with whom I have spent innumerable happy, if often wet, hours in the Lake District on day trips and longer holidays. It came to a head in 2001 when we spent a week at Tallantire, near Cockermouth, a bit away from our usual haunts. We kept passing places like Dearham, Maryport and Silloth and I would be boring her stupid by pointing out that Alvin Ackerley came from here and that James Lomas was born there and that Jim Brough played on that pitch. We would approach Egremont and I would ask her why there was no statue to Martin Hodgson, not that I expected an answer, as she had absolutely no idea who he was, apart from knowing that he must be a Rugby League player. Anyway, she was far more interested in trips to Lakeland Plastics in Windermere or to that sublime chocolate shop in Keswick or to Hayes Garden Centre in Ambleside.

The fact that the whole area was marked by placenames which evoked thoughts or memories of living or long-dead Rugby League players, such as Bill Kirkbride, Stan Satterthwaite or – how Cumbrian can a name get? – James Wasdale Brough, simply emphasised the idea that these notable men should be commemorated and this book is the result.

Selection of the one hundred players included was difficult and some fine players who are not included could just as easily have been. It is certainly true that 130 into 100 does not go. I would have dearly liked to have found space for such men as Billy Hannah, Frank Spottiswoode, Bill Nanson, Tom Fenwick, Frank Longman, Jimmy Wareing and Joe Bonnar, to name but a few.

Of course, the term 'great' is grossly over-used and strictly is not applicable to all the personalities in this book. Some were by any measure among the greats of the sport, while over half were test players, international caps or Lions tourists. Whatever their perceived status, all were definitely notable in some respect and all upheld the traditional values of Cumbrian Rugby League.

I have deliberately not included any current players. Indeed, very few would be considered worthy. The truth of the matter is that club Rugby League in Cumbria has not produced a native-born test player since Whitehaven's Vince Gribbin won his only cap in 1985. Workington Town, once a heavy producer of test players, has not supplied a native Cumbrian to the Great Britain side since Eddie Bowman in 1977.

This lack of star production is sadly symptomatic of the state of Rugby League in the county. Although amateur Rugby League remains strong in the area, it is not as strong as it used to be. There have been well-publicised fears about falling numbers of players in the traditionally strongest districts of West Cumbria and further south the Barrow League has experienced severe difficulties.

Problems in the professional game, greatly exacerbated since the arrival of Super League, have been almost terminal. Whitehaven and Workington languish in the NFP and can raise little more than a thousand spectators between them on a weekend. Carlisle have folded but ludicrously purported to have merged with Barrow. A couple of years ago all hell was let loose when it seemed that the Rugby League authorities had earmarked Workington Town for expulsion. Fortunately, it did not happen but, do not be fooled, one day it might.

Overall it is a dismal scene. The powers that run the game occasionally claim to have Cumbria in their hearts and on their minds, but do precious little in practice. The truth is that when Rugby League was a part-time sport, small-town clubs like 'Haven and Town could hope for a place among the elite. Super League is not about small-town clubs and part-time players. The trouble with Cumbrians is that there are too few of them. Even combined Whitehaven and Workington have a population of around 50,000, simply not enough for the moguls who run Super League. They do not want franchise applications from areas of such limited catchment.

Another problem for Rugby League in the area is the lack of local incentive for aspiring and established players. There has not been an inter-county game since 30 May 1982, when Lancashire hammered Cumbria at Derwent Park. There have, of course, been one-off games against touring teams – ten, in fact, in twenty years, most of them involving heavy defeats by the Kangaroos and Kiwis. Naturally, such games are a welcome opportunity for players to test themselves against the best and for local fans to see the best. However, it is all rather cosmetic. The Cumbrians are usually drawn from clubs outside Super League and resemble sacrificial lambs.

Let us hope that the game in Cumbria can somehow regain its former status and glories. Until then we can at least remember the greats of the past.

Acknowledgements

I am particularly indebted to Mike Gardner of the *News & Star* in Carlisle and to Cumbrian Newspapers for permission to use some of their photographs. Some of the profiles in this book are abridged versions of articles originally written for and published in the *News & Star* in 1999.

Sam Coulter, renowned for his collection of Cumbrian Rugby League memorabilia, has also been most generous in providing many images which would otherwise have proved impossible to acquire. I am also grateful to Bill Nelson, another avid Cumbrian collector, and to the following: Rodney Bradshaw, Tony Capstick, Hazel Carlton, Andrew Cudbertson, John Edwards, Craig Evans, Raymond Fletcher, Charles Gate, Andrew Hardcastle, Dot Little, Dave Makin, Keith Nutter, Bob Shuttleworth, Michael Turner, Brian Walker, Andrew Wheelwright and Steve Wild.

Most of the images in this book are derived from private collections. It has not been possible to ascertain the origins in some cases. If copyrights have been infringed, it has been unintentional.

The statistics contained in this work have for the most part been derived from the works of the Rugby League Record Keepers Club, sadly now defunct. In some respects they may, therefore, differ from other published sources.

The Cumberland team which beat Glamorgan & Monmouthshire 15-5 at Whitehaven on 20 October 1928. Players from left to right, back row: H. Young, D. Clark, O. Errington, M. Strong, M. Hodgson, A. Troup. Front row: E. Thornburrow, T. Holliday, F. Southward, R. Scott, J. Coulson, J. Oliver, J. Brough.

In 1972 the last true Cumberland county team took the field beating Yorkshire 23-14 at Whitehaven and losing 16-26 to Lancashire at Warrington. From 1973 onwards, local government reorganisation meant that a wider Cumbria replaced the old county. From left to right, back row: R. Thompson, L. Gorley, T. Thompson, E. Bowman, R. Morton, J. Pringle, G. Kirkpatrick, A. Colloby, R. Nicholson senior. Front row: M. Gracey, R. Nicholson junior, P. Kitchin, P. Charlton, J. McFarlane, F. Foster, J. Bonnar, R. Morris.

100 Cumberland Greats

Alvin Ackerley
Howard Allen
Harry Archer
Colin Armstrong
Fred Ashworth
Jeff Bawden
Les Bettinson
Eddie Bowman
Jim Brough
Paul Charlton
James Clampitt
Richard Clampitt
Douglas Clark
Geoff Clark
Tony Colloby
Gordon Cottier
Jack Coulson
Paddy Dalton
Billy Dixon
Bill Drake
Jim Drake
Bill Eagers
Brian Edgar
Joe Ferguson
Billy Fisher
Tom Fletcher
Jack Flynn
Frank Foster
Tom Gainford
Billy Garratt
Eppie Gibson
Les Gorley
Peter Gorley
Vince Gribbin
Jimmy Hayton
John Henderson
Martin Hodgson

Billy Holding
Bill Holliday
Les Holliday
Tom Holliday
Dick Huddart
Hudson Irving
Billy Ivison
Bill Kirkbride
Billy Kitchin
Phil Kitchin
Jim Lewthwaite
Billy Little
Sid Little
William B Little
James Lomas
Syd Lowdon
Bill Martin
Bill McAlone
Alan McCurrie
John McFarlane
Danny McKeating
Vince McKeating
John McKeown
Jimmy Metcalfe
Sammy Miller
Bob Nicholson
Sammy Northmore
John O'Neill
Joe Oliver
Joe Owens
Geoff Palmer
Kevin Pape
Jimmy Parkinson
Bill Pattinson
Billy Pattinson
Albert Pepperell
Russ Pepperell

Stanley Pepperell
Johnny Rae
John Risman
James Ritson
Geoff Robinson
John Roper
Stan Satterthwaite
Bobby Scott
Bill Smith
Fergie Southward
Ike Southward
Jack Stoddart
Miller Strong
John Tembey
Ted Thornburrow
Alec Troup
Arnie Walker
Syd Walmsley
Billy Ward
Silas Warwick
Ivor Watts
Billy Wedgwood
Billy Winskill
Ian Wright
Joe Wright
Harold Young

The twenty who appear here in **bold**, occupy two pages instead of the usual one.

Alvin Ackerley
Hooker

First-class debut*
6 April 1946,
Workington Town v. Hunslet (home)
Last game
23 April 1962,
Hull KR v. Wakefield Trinity (away)
Cumberland debut
26 September 1946,
v. Yorkshire at Workington
Cumberland caps
16, 1946-59
England caps
6
Test caps
2
Clubs
Workington Town, Halifax, Hull KR

*Ackerley played for Barrow v. Hunslet as a trialist on 7 April 1945

The most recent generation of Rugby League fans has grown up with no concept of what a real hooker is. The last decade has seen the scrummage rendered redundant. It no longer serves any real purpose. Anybody's granny could be stuck in the middle of the front row and the team putting the ball in would win the scrum. Scrummaging now entails no skills at all and no forward expends an ounce of energy in the whole business.

How different it was in the old days. Hookers were a breed on their own, consumed with one thought – getting the ball. Few ever got the ball as well as Alvin Ackerley. In the entire history of the game only four hookers have played in over 600 games. 'Ack' was one. He must therefore have packed down in close on 30,000 scrums and he certainly won a lot more strikes than he lost.

Alvin Ackerley was born in Dearham in 1927 and he came from rugby-playing stock. Indeed his first junior club, Broughton Moor, had had Ackerleys in their ranks for decades before he was born and for a game in early 1945 Broughton Moor was reported to have fielded Alvin and ten other Ackerleys or their blood relations.

Alvin signed as a professional for Workington Town in their inaugural season,

making his first-team debut in an 8-0 victory over Hunslet at Borough Park on 6 April 1946. In the next two and a half years he played 72 games for Town before falling out with player-manager Gus Risman. He briefly went back to playing as an amateur for Brookland Rovers before being signed by Halifax in October 1948. It was as a Halifax player that he made his name as one of the most effective hookers the game has produced.

Halifax finished fifth from bottom of the league in Alvin's first season at Thrum Hall but pulled off one of the surprises of the century in reaching the 1949 Challenge Cup final, meeting near neighbours and arch-rivals Bradford Northern, who were playing in their third consecutive Wembley final. Northern were a much better team than Halifax but were extremely worried about Alvin's ability to dominate possession. In the event Halifax lost 0-12 and after the game Alvin, nursing a painfully swollen, possibly broken, hand, complained bitterly to a Halifax director that it had been trodden on by Frank Whitcombe, Northern's 18st prop. The director had little sympathy replying, 'Happen he wouldn't have trodden on it, if you hadn't been hooking with it!'

That was Alvin all right, but like any good hooker in those times Alvin would do almost anything to win the ball. That was his job and scrummaging was no place for fainthearts.

Halifax developed a pack in the early and mid-1950s to rival any the game has seen. It was supremely fit, ferocious, focused and full of hard and, some said, ruthless men. At times there were seven international or test players vying for only six places. It swept them to Wembley in 1954 and 1956, to the Championship finals of 1953, 1954 and 1956 and Alvin Ackerley was its leader.

He was an unlikely leader – short and squat at 5ft 7in, 13st 7lbs and possessing a high-pitched, squeaky voice. However, he led by example and was as hard as nails. His pack followed him everywhere. He was a clever player, too. He was the very devil at dummy-half, adept at selling the dummy and fond of the odd mischievous grubber kick. He captained Halifax through the 1952/53 to 1955/56 seasons and was the darling of the Halifax crowd. Forty-odd years on, his name is still revered in Halifax.

Those five Challenge Cup and Championship finals brought only disappointment as Halifax lost them all, several desperately unluckily. In the Championship finals of 1954 and 1956 they scored more tries than their opponents, Warrington and Hull, but lost to late penalty goals on both occasions, whilst in the 1954 Challenge Cup final they lost narrowly in the celebrated Odsal replay to Warrington. That replay drew an official world record crowd of 102,569 to Bradford, although there were certainly tens of thousands more present. Alvin had played before the previous world record crowd too – the 1949 Wembley final which drew 95,000.

There were, however, winners' medals for 'Ack'. He captained Halifax in their victorious Yorkshire Cup finals against Hull in 1954, when he scored a rare try, and again in 1955. In addition he earned Yorkshire League Championship winners' medals in 1952/53, 1953/54, 1955/56 and 1957/58.

In representative rugby Alvin was a Cumberland cap before he was nineteen, possibly a record for a hooker, and he played for the county for thirteen years. He won half a dozen England caps, helping England to share the International Championship in 1952/53 and to win it in 1953/54. In 1952 he was a member of the Ashes-winning Great Britain team. He was a mystifying omission from the 1954 Australasian tour party but belatedly became a Lion on the 1958 tour.

Alvin left Halifax in 1959 having played in 396 games for the club. His final move was to Hull KR for whom he played until 1962, rattling up exactly 100 appearances for them.

Alvin Ackerley died in 1973, aged only forty-six. He had certainly made his mark as a Rugby League great from coast to coast. He was arguably the most successful hooker Cumberland has produced.

Howard Allen
Hooker

First-class debut
16 January 1965,
Workington Town v. Salford (away)
Last game
25 October 1981,
Workington Town v. Batley (home)
Cumberland debut
25 October 1967, v. Yorkshire at Castleford
Cumberland caps
10, 1967-74
Clubs
Workington Town, Blackpool Borough,
Barrow

Howard Allen was popularly known as 'Smiler' Allen. No matter how rough the going got, and Howard was usually in the middle of things, there would be the grinning face of Smiler, infuriating his opponents, geeing up his colleagues and either endearing himself to or provoking the fans. In popular parlance he was 'a right character'.

Smiler was a product of Kells and signed for Workington Town in 1964. He was a hooker, who hooked as well as any of his contemporaries and did his share of the tackling. However, as he got older he got craftier. He knew all the tricks and became extremely adept at winning crucial games, either through his chicanery at the play-the-ball or through his penchant for dropping goals.

He was in good company from the start at Workington. In his debut, a 7-7 draw at Salford, his props were the redoubtable Martin brothers. It took Smiler three seasons to establish himself as Town's hooker as Malcolm Moss needed a lot of shifting from the job. Later on he had to contend with Alan Banks for the role. Although Smiler played for ten years at Derwent Park, he got no nearer to a major final than four Lancashire Cup semifinals (1967, 1973, 1974, 1975) and the semifinal of the ill-fated Captain Morgan Trophy in 1973/74.

When he moved to Blackpool Borough for £1,000 in 1976, most pundits did not regard it as a good career move. Smiler flourished, however. A try on his debut at Hull was soon followed by a virtuoso performance, as he scored all three tries in Borough's 19-16

victory at Huyton on 14 March 1976. The following season Smiler was the star of Blackpool's amazing surge to the final of the John Player Trophy, one of the most popular and romantic achievements in the game's history. Howard scored vital points in all five rounds – a drop goal in a 16-15 win against Barrow; another as Halifax were beaten 7-3; typically, two tries at Workington and another in the semi-final against Leigh. The fairy tale ended in the final against Castleford but Smiler scored another try and won, jointly, the man of the match award.

He never played again for Blackpool. Instead he moved to Barrow, where he carried on in the same vein, helping the team to promotion in 1977/78 and 1979/80. In 1980/81 he appeared in another John Player final, as his team confounded the critics. In the semi-final, Smiler scored the winning try ten minutes from time as Hull were surprised 13-10 but Barrow went down 5-12 to Warrington in the final at Wigan. A week later Smiler scored all three Barrow tries in a 15-8 win at Oldham.

He ended his career with a short loan spell back at Workington in 1981. His career record read 384 games, 71 tries and 41 goals.

Harry Archer

Stand-off

First-class debut
4 April 1953, Workington Town v. Rochdale Hornets (home)
Last game
15 April 1967,
Whitehaven v. Liverpool City (home)
Cumberland debut
19 September 1955,
v. Lancashire at Workington
Cumberland caps
13, 1955-66
Clubs
Workington Town, Whitehaven

Only Paul Charlton and John Roper have given Workington Town more service in terms of match appearances than Harry Archer, who played 387 games between 1953 and 1967. That record is its own eloquent testimony.

Harry was a stand-off with Workington RU club – the 'Zebras' – before joining Town, although he had played league for his native Dearham. He was heftier than most conventional league stand-offs at 13st 8lbs and he played a robust game, being especially strong in the tackle. He was not merely a stopper, however, for he played with his brain and had fine handling and kicking skills, which set up many a try for his colleagues.

Of course, he is mainly remembered for his long and bewildering half-back partnership with Sol Roper. The two were first paired on 24 September 1955 in a 29-15 success at Dewsbury and the following week played together against the New Zealanders. For more than a decade and well over 300 matches, the two seemed indivisible. They did not score many tries, Harry claiming just 64 for Town, but created hundreds.

Harry began his Town career at the close of the 1952/53 season and finished on the losing side five times in his first six games. It was 1955/56 before he established himself as Town's permanent number six and it was in

the same season that he made his Cumberland debut, scoring a try against Lancashire at Derwent Park. He also played against Yorkshire in 1955, along with Roper, but did not get another cap until 1961. Thereafter he was a regular, gaining County Championship winners' medals in 1961/62, 1963/64, 1965/66 and 1966/67.

In 1958 he won his highest honour. He was selected in the second tour trial at Leeds on 19 March and scored a rare hat-trick playing outside Alec Murphy, as the Greens beat the Whites 41-18. Harry and Wigan's Dave Bolton were chosen as the Lions stand-offs for Australasia. However, the tour was spoiled for Harry by a succession of injuries and he only played in seven games in Australia and one in New Zealand.

Workington reached both the Challenge Cup final and Championship final in 1958, Harry being a major factor in getting them there. Town lost 9-13 at Wembley to Wigan, injuries playing a big part. Harry was knocked senseless by a high Mick Sullivan tackle early in the game and was not his usual effective self. A Championship runners-up medal was all he got the following week too, when Hull beat Town 20-3 at Odsal, as the Cumbrians played with twelve men for 55 minutes. He had to wait until 1962 before picking up a winner's medal, when Town won the Western Division Championship.

Harry played his last game for Town on 19 November 1966 against Huddersfield before joining Whitehaven, for whom he made seven appearances before retiring.

Colin Armstrong
Prop forward

First-class debut
2 September 1984,
Carlisle v. Doncaster (home)
Last game
9 April 2000, Whitehaven v. Featherstone
Rovers (away)
Cumbria debut
19 October 1988 v. France at Whitehaven
Cumbria caps
6, 1988-94
Clubs
Carlisle, Hull KR, Workington Town,
Swinton, Whitehaven

Colin Armstrong's career covered most of the 1980s, the 1990s and ended in 2000. It encompassed 480 matches, which is a colossal achievement for a player in modern times, when fewer games are played. Moreover, he played most of his games at prop, although he could cover second row, which is eloquent testimony to his durability. A very big man at 6ft 3in and 15st 10lbs (1991 figures), Colin was an astute ball-handler, a good defender and a useful goal-kicker.

An amateur with Broughton Red Rose, Colin had trials with Workington Town but signed for Carlisle. He made his debut, along with Kevin Pape, in a 31-15 home defeat of Doncaster on the opening day of the 1984/85 season and landed a goal. He stayed at Carlisle for over four years, making 106 appearances, in which he scored 60 points.

Colin moved to Hull Kingston Rovers, for whom he made his debut in a 24-60 loss at Warrington on 8 January 1989. Rovers were relegated but in 1989/90 lifted the Second Division Championship and were runners-up in the Second Division Premiership final to Oldham, who beat them 30-29 in an enthralling encounter at Old Trafford. It was the first of three Old Trafford finals for Colin. In one of his last games for Rovers on 19 August 1990, Colin kicked fourteen goals in a 100-6 mauling of Nottingham City in a Yorkshire Cup-tie, played bizarrely at Doncaster, to equal the club record.

In 1990 Colin joined Workington Town for a seven-season stint, becoming captain and leading them to a Divisional Premiership final in 1993, when they lost 16-20 to Featherstone, and to a 30-22 victory over London Crusaders in the Second Division Premiership final in 1994. Promotion to Division One was also won.

After 196 games (28 tries, 45 goals, 198 points) for Workington Town, he moved briefly to Swinton in 1996 (18 games) but returned to Cumbria in 1997, playing the 1997, 1998 and 2000 seasons for Whitehaven (69 games, 46 points) and the 1999 season for Workington Town (30 games, one try). Remarkably, he did not miss a game in either 1998 or 1999.

Apart from his three Old Trafford finals and Second Division Championships with Hull KR and Workington, Colin did not win any major domestic honours in his monumental but labyrinthine career. He did, however, play for Cumbria on six occasions, beginning with an 18-13 victory over France at Whitehaven in 1988. He also played three times for Cumbria against the Australians, all heavy defeats, and once against the New Zealanders, when he kicked a goal in a 2-28 reverse at Whitehaven. He scored his solitary try for the county in a 34-12 success against Papua-New Guinea at Derwent Park in 1991.

Fred Ashworth

Second rower, prop

First-class debut
2 October 1926, Oldham v. Barrow (home)
Last game
27 December 1938,
Oldham v. Rochdale Hornets (home)
Cumberland debut
23 March 1927, v. Lancashire at Salford
Cumberland caps
13, 1927-31
Club
Oldham

To play 436 games for one club in twelve years is a genuine feat of endurance, reflecting enormous stamina, high fitness levels and exceptional loyalty. They were all qualities displayed in superabundance by Fred Ashworth, who left Aspatria to join Oldham in 1926. Fred was a second-rower and prop, at 5ft 11in and 13st 7lbs, a fine all-round forward, powerful and direct on attack and a stern tackler, who did his whack in the scrums.

Although still in his teens he began his Oldham career in the front row. On only his fourth appearance he was pitted against the touring Kiwis, who were beaten 15-10 with Fred scoring the first of his 39 tries for the club. Three years later, on 2 November 1929, he was in the Oldham team which beat the Australians 10-8, a game he regarded as the hardest of his career.

Fred's first season ended wonderfully. Oldham fought their way through to the Challenge Cup final, beating Swinton 26-7 at Wigan. Fred figured in all the Cup rounds and played a leading part in a pack that ultimately dominated the formidable Swinton forwards. It was, however, his last Challenge Cup final, as Oldham gradually declined. In 1929 and

1930, Fred played in losing Lancashire Cup semi-finals and in 1931 in a losing Championship semi-final at Swinton.

1933/34 saw a resurgence in the club's fortunes and Fred took a Lancashire Cup-winner's medal, when Oldham beat St Helens Recs 12-0 in the final at Swinton. He almost got to Wembley a few months later, but Widnes edged out Oldham 7-4 in the Challenge Cup semi-final.

On 17 September 1934, Fred scored a try in Oldham's breathtaking 26-25 victory against Villeneuve, the first French club to tour England. Apart from scoring the odd try, Fred occasionally kicked goals, landing 38 for Oldham. His best haul was 26 in his last full season, 1937/38, including five in a 22-0 win against St Helens Recs at Watersheddings and three in a 6-10 defeat by the Kangaroos.

Fred never quite made international status but he came close in 1932, when he played in a tour trial at Fartown, along with his Oldham colleagues, stand-off Jack Oster and centre Jack Stephens. Surprisingly, his county career only lasted four years but he squeezed in thirteen appearances. He made his debut in a 5-12 defeat by Lancashire at Salford on 23 March 1927, in a team that included Oldham players Tom Holliday and Bert Lister.

His second season with Cumberland, 1927/28, brought victories over Lancashire, Glamorgan & Monmouth and Yorkshire and provided him with a County Championship-winner's medal. In 1929 he was on the winning side against the Australians at Workington. In most of his Cumberland appearances he formed a terrific second-row pairing with Martin Hodgson.

Jeff Bawden
Winger, centre

First-class debut
23 October 1943,
Huddersfield v. Hull (home) Yorkshire Cup
Last game
20 December 1952,
Huddersfield v. Leigh (home)
Cumberland debut
31 October 1945 v. Yorkshire at Leeds
Cumberland caps
14, 1945-52
Club
Huddersfield

Jeffrey Bawden was born in Whitehaven in 1924. At thirteen he played Rugby Union for England Schoolboys against Wales at Cardiff Arms Park. Later he played soccer for Kells Boys Club and Rugby League for Hensingham. He was such a good soccer player that Wolverhampton Wanderers offered him trials but he opted to join Huddersfield on 23 October 1943.

Quickly he established himself as Huddersfield's left-winger and was a determined and regular try-scorer. His weaponry was augmented, moreover, with a propensity for kicking goals with unerring regularity with his left foot. Huddersfield won the Challenge Cup final in 1945 with Jeff providing 43 of the 83 points in the eight ties they played.

In the first leg at Fartown, Huddersfield won 7-4 in a blizzard, Jeff's conversion and penalty materially influencing the result. In the second leg at Odsal almost equally atrocious conditions prevailed. When Bradford led 5-0 in the second half it looked as if the Cup would be theirs. Jeff Bawden had other ideas. Following a scrum on the Bradford line the ball went out to the left wing allowing Jeff to force his way over. Ten minutes from time he settled matters when Northern's passing broke down and he cleverly dribbled the ball to the line to score again. Huddersfield won 6-5.

The immediate post-war seasons saw Jeff in prime form. In 1945/46 he amassed 239 points to top the league's scoring charts, while his total of 85 goals was second only to Dewsbury's Jimmy Ledgard's 89. In one game against Swinton he piled up 35 points from five tries and ten goals as Huddersfield won 76-3. Two days later he scored 20 points in a 43-5 victory over Barrow. Many judges thought him unlucky to be overlooked for the 1946 Lions tour, although he did play in a tour trial at Wigan on 30 January 1946.

Jeff played in the 1946 Championship final against Wigan at Maine Road, kicking two goals as Huddersfield lost 4-13. In 1946/47 he again topped the scoring charts with 246 points, finishing second in 1947/48 with 261 and third in 1948/49 with 221. He had proved to be one of the most consistent match-winners of his era as those first four post-war seasons saw him rattle up almost 1,000 points. By then he had settled at centre.

Jeff earned a Championship winners' medal in 1948/49 and a runners-up medal the following season. He won Yorkshire League Championships with the Fartowners in both those seasons and played for Huddersfield in the Yorkshire Cup final of 1949 when they were defeated by Bradford Northern. His Fartown career yielded 243 games and 1,303 points.

A regular for Cumberland for seven years, Jeff proved his outstanding versatility by figuring at wing, centre, full-back and stand-off.

First-class debut
9 March 1957, Salford v. Batley (home)
Last game
10 September 1969, Salford v. Wigan (home)
Cumberland debut
11 September 1957 v. Yorkshire at Hull
Cumberland caps
7, 1957-67
Club
Salford

Les scored the first of his 75 tries for Salford in a 11-10 defeat at Blackpool on 7 March 1959, and was top try-scorer with eleven in 1966/67. He also kicked ten goals for the club. His best points haul in a game was sixteen (five goals, two tries), also against Blackpool at The Willows on 11 April 1964, in a 25-8 success.

Salford were not a successful team during Les's career. The nearest he got to a medal was a couple of appearances in Lancashire Cup semi-finals. However, he was still a first-teamer when the club laid the foundations for the great team of the early 1970s, so he played alongside such luminaries as David Watkins and Chris Hesketh.

Les won seven caps for Cumberland, all as a centre, and in five of those games his wingers scored tries. He was twice a member of a County Championship-winning team – in 1965/66 and 1966/67.

When Les finished playing in 1969, he stayed on as a coach. In 1973/74 he succeeded Cliff Evans as first-team coach and presided over a period of immense success until 1977. Salford were champions in 1973/74 and 1975/76, Premiership runners-up in 1975/76, Lancashire Cup finalists in 1974 and 1975 and lifted the BBC2 Floodlit Trophy in 1974/75, when Warrington were beaten 15-10 in the final after a 0-0 draw.

On finishing coaching in 1977, Les served for fourteen years on the Salford board. He became Great Britain manager in 1985 and led the 1988 Lions to Australia and New Zealand. In December 1989, he was controversially replaced by Maurice Lindsay. Les was made president of the RFL in 1988/89, a richly deserved honour.

As a seventeen year old playing amateur Rugby League for Millom, Les Bettinson nearly became a Workington Town player in 1952, when Gus Risman persuaded him to trial at Derwent Park. Les eventually did sign for Gus, but not until 1957 when he was managing Salford. At that time Les was playing for Millom RU club, having retained his amateur status while completing his teacher training course.

Les's relationship with Salford would continue for the next thirty-four years, twelve of them as a player of great versatility. His career at the Willows began with a 16-5 home victory over Batley on 9 March 1957 but he did not really establish himself as a first-team regular until the 1960/61 season. Although he is often remembered primarily as a centre, Les gave sterling service all over the back division. Of his 317 full appearances (he also played twice as a substitute) 108 were at left centre, 65 at right centre, 65 at right wing, 22 at left wing, 43 at stand-off and 14 at full-back, indicating just what a good all-round practitioner he was.

Eddie Bowman

Second-rower, prop,

First-class debut
20 August 1966, Whitehaven v. Batley (away)
Last game
8 November 1981, Wigan v. York (away)
Cumberland debut
24 September 1969,
v. Lancashire at Workington
Cumberland caps
8, 1969-75
Test caps
4
Clubs
Whitehaven, Workington Town, Leigh, Wigan

Kells have produced innumerable top class players and one of the very best was Eddie Bowman, who played at professional level for fifteen years. His first senior club was Whitehaven, for whom he scored nineteen tries in 69 appearances (1966-69). Big, a six footer, over 14st and mobile, Eddie was a real eye-catcher with a hard running style in his early years at the Recreation Ground.

A move to Workington Town in 1970, however, brought out the creativity in his play. He was a superb ball-distributor, whose subtle skills made other players look better. Eddie put in eight years at Derwent Park, gradually moving from second-row to blindside prop as Town began to challenge for honours. In 1973, 1974 and 1975 he played in three losing Lancashire Cup semi-finals but gained compensation when Town won promotion in 1975/76. He then figured in three consecutive Lancashire Cup finals, collecting runners-up medals in 1976 and 1978 against Widnes but putting on a fabulous virtuoso display in 1977, when Wigan were defeated 16-13 at Warrington.

On 22 October, two weeks after the 1978 final, Eddie played his 199th and last game (25 tries, two goals) for Workington in a 13-5 home defeat by Wakefield Trinity. He was transferred to Leigh for £7,500, making his debut on 10 December in a 15-10 loss to Wakefield at Hilton Park. His stay at Leigh was pretty unproductive and in almost two years he made only 36 appearances, playing his last game against the 1980 New Zealanders.

His final move was to Wigan, who had fallen into the Second Division. He made his debut in a 15-2 home victory over newcomers Fulham on 30 November 1980 and helped the Cherry and Whites to promotion at the first attempt.

Eddie made his Cumberland debut, while still a Whitehaven player, against Lancashire at Workington in 1969, sharing the second-row duties with his team-mate Tom Gainford. He made eight appearances for Cumberland, including one as a substitute, and he scored three tries – against Lancashire in 1972 at Warrington and against Yorkshire at Dewsbury and Other Nationalities at Barrow in 1975. His seven starts were all made as a second-rower and he had seven different partners – Gainford, Bill Kirkbride, Harold McCourt, Rod Smith, Spanky McFarlane, Les Gorley and Bob Blackwood.

Eddie was playing some of the best football of his life as he neared the end of his time at Workington and the test selectors finally recognised the fact by picking him for the World Cup squad to Australasia in 1977. Although he was now a regular prop, Britain used him as a second row with George Nicholls. The pair were sensational, Eddie playing in all four Cup games and in five of the other seven tour fixtures. Britain lost the World Cup final 13-12 to Australia.

First-class debut
2 September 1925, Leeds v. York (home)
Last game
8 April 1944, Leeds v. Wigan (home)
Cumberland debut
29 October 1925, v. Yorkshire at Huddersfield
Cumberland caps
24, 1925-36
England caps
11
Test caps
5
Club
Leeds

It is safe to say that Cumberland has provided Rugby League with two truly world class full-backs, men worthy to be ranked with the very best from any era. Workington's Paul Charlton certainly falls into this category and will have been seen in his pomp by many readers of this book. Was Paul, however, better than James Wasdale Brough?

Of course, the question is unanswerable. Both were similarly magnificent running full-backs but in vastly different eras.

Jim Brough was born in Silloth in 1903 and was originally a fisherman. He did not play a game of Rugby League until he was almost twenty-two but had already made his name as a Rugby Union star. Surprisingly, in view of its isolation and lack of major clubs, Cumberland was a major Rugby Union power in the early 1920s and Jim Brough was a key member of the side that won the County Championship by defeating Kent 14-3 in the final at Carlisle in 1924. On 3 January 1925, he turned out for England against New Zealand at Twickenham before a crowd of 60,000, one of the great occasions in English Rugby Union's history. His side lost 17-11 but two weeks later at the same venue he was in the XV which defeated Wales 12-6.

His next international appearance would be a lot nearer home and as a professional. A proces-

sion of Rugby League clubs, as well as Liverpool AFC, beat a path to his door before, on 29 June 1925, he finally accepted an offer of £600 to join Leeds. Club and player lived happily ever after, or at least until Jim finally retired in 1944, having passed his fortieth birthday.

Jim made his debut as a Loiner on 2 September 1925 in a 13-9 home win against York. He was a natural. Rugby League suited his adventurous style although full-backs in those days were not expected to be significant attacking figures. He could perform all the traditional tasks expected of the pre-war full-back in that his defence was deadly, his catching was flawless, he was a prodigious left-footed punter of the ball and he could kick goals when necessary. It was, however, his willingness to attack from the back that made Jim Brough such an outstanding player.

Gus Risman, a Cumbrian legend in his own right, once wrote, 'Jim Brough was probably the finest of all attacking full-backs. He was such a good attacker that he was just as good a player at centre-three-quarter as he was at full-back. His speed was phenomenal.' There could be no better qualified judge than Risman.

Jim's brilliance as an attacking player is reflected in his long and distinguished career with Cumberland. He made his county debut against Lancashire at Whitehaven only 24 days after playing his first game for Leeds. He went on to make 24 appearances for Cumberland over a dozen seasons but only played full-back on his debut. Twenty-two of his caps were won at centre while he played at stand-off in a famous victory over the

Australians at Workington in 1929.

It was, however, the following encounter with the Kangaroos at Whitehaven's Recreation Ground on 9 December 1933, which probably provided his most memorable moment as a Cumberland player. Jim was in his first season as captain of the county and had led his team to the County Championship with a victory over Yorkshire just three days earlier. The Australians had already easily beaten both Lancashire and Yorkshire and with five minutes remaining they were leading the Cumbrians 16-12. At that point second-rower Alec Troup (Barrow) scored an unconverted try to make the score 16-15.

Amidst nerve-snapping tension, the Cumbrians fought tooth and nail to steal the game. Four minutes into injury time Jim Brough, who had already scored a miraculous try at the start of the second half, found himself with the ball 40 yards from the Australian posts and let fly with a cannon-ball drop at goal. It was the last act of a match as enthralling as any the county has ever witnessed. As the ball bisected the posts the ground erupted in celebration of Cumberland's historic 17-16 victory.

The Recreation Ground had also been the scene of Jim's introduction to international football on 4 February 1926. That day saw a new grandstand opened as well as the first encounter at this exalted level between Jim and his greatest rival, Wigan's Welsh genius, Jim Sullivan. On this occasion Jim Brough had most to smile about as England defeated Other Nationalities

37-11. Jim would win eleven caps for England (1926-36), appear in only one losing team and captain his country four times.

Whilst all Jim's games for England were played in his normal position of full-back, Jim Sullivan was immovable from the number one jersey in the test XIII for most of Brough's career. That did not, however, stop the great Cumbrian from touring Australasia in 1928 and forcing his way into the test team at centre on four occasions, as the Lions won both series against Australia and New Zealand. In 1936 Jim Brough became only the second Cumbrian to captain a Lions tour, although injuries restricted him to only one test when he led his team to a 12-7 victory at Brisbane to square the series.

At club level Jim enjoyed wonderful success. With Leeds he won five Yorkshire Cup finals and six Yorkshire League Championships and he played in three Challenge Cup finals in 1932, 1936 and 1942, all of which were won. He was captain in the latter two. His career with Leeds did not end until April 1944, by which time he had played a monumental 442 games for the Loiners in which he had scored 37 tries and 84 goals.

When his playing days were over, Jim Brough continued to achieve great things in the game. He coached Leeds, Workington Town and Whitehaven. As successor to Gus Risman at Workington he led the club to Wembley in 1955 and 1958, whilst in the latter year he made his third Lions tour, this time as coach.

First-class debut
23 September 1961, Workington Town v.
Rochdale Hornets (away)
Last game
20 April 1981,
Blackpool Borough v. Wigan (home)
Cumberland debut
8 September 1965, v. Yorkshire at Hull KR
Cumberland caps
32, 1965-79
England caps
1
Test caps
19
Clubs
Workington Town, Salford, Blackpool
Borough

Paul Charlton is arguably the finest full-back to have been produced in Cumberland and that is saying a great deal when his predecessors included such wonderful players as Billy Little, Bill Eagers, Bobbie Scott, Jim Brough, Billy Holding, John McKeown and Syd Lowdon. Certainly, as an attacking, try-scoring full-back, the region has never seen his equal and, if he were playing in the modern game, he would be in his element – without doubt in the superstar bracket.

After joining Workington Town from Kells in 1960, Paul launched a career at the top level that was truly monumental in achievement. His debut for Town at first-team level came on 23 September 1961 in a 14-4 victory at Rochdale Hornets, when he filled in for Syd Lowdon. It was not until the 1963/64 season, however, that Paul made the Workington full-back spot his own. Thereafter he was immovable from the number one jersey wherever he plied his trade.

Paul soon forced his way into the Cumberland team, making his debut in a 19-3 win over Yorkshire at Craven Park, Hull on 8 September 1965. Cumberland lifted the County Championship that season and repeated the success the following season, Paul being ever-present. His career in the county colours was to stretch until 5 September 1979, when he substituted for John Risman in a 15-23 defeat by Lancashire at St Helens. It was his 32nd cap. He had captained Cumberland on 20 occasions.

Within a month of making his county debut, Paul Charlton became a test player when he appeared for Great Britain in a 15-9 triumph over New Zealand at Odsal on 23 October 1965. It was, however, to be another five years before he would don a test jersey again. There were some fine full-backs in his way, notably Arthur Keegan (Hull), Ken Gowers (Swinton), Bev Risman (Leeds), Ray Dutton (Widnes) and Derek Edwards (Castleford). It was not until the World Cup of 1970 and another encounter with the Kiwis that he would reappear in the red, white and blue and then it was as a substitute in Britain's 27-17 victory.

At club level Paul was attracting rave reviews. By 1969 he had already played 244 games for Town, piling up 391 points from 79 tries and 77 goals. It was no surprise that he became a target for the glamour club of the period, Brian Snape's Salford. A world record cash transfer fee of £12,500 exchanged hands between Town and the Red Devils in October 1969 and Paul became one of the game's greatest stars. He made his debut for Salford on 29 October 1979 in a 16-12 home win against St Helens.

In 234 games for Salford in his six-year stint at The Willows he plundered 99 tries. Included among them were a phenomenal 31 touchdowns (plus two in representative games) in the 1972/73 season, which created a world record for a full-back. It comprehensively smashed Colin Tyrer's previous record of 21 set four years earlier. Salford were Rugby League Champions in 1973/74 and Paul won a Lancashire Cup-winner's medal in 1972, when he scored a try in a 25-11 victory over Swinton at Warrington. He also played in beaten Salford sides in the Lancashire Cup finals of 1973 and 1974. In the Players Trophy final of 1973 he also had to settle for a loser's medal,

as Leeds beat the Red Devils 12-7 in a gripping game at Fartown. In 1974/75, he played in the BBC2 Floodlit Trophy final against Warrington at Salford, which ended scoreless. He missed the replay at Wilderspool, which Salford won 15-10, but was entitled to a winner's medal.

Paul's career for Great Britain took off when he joined Salford. Between 1972 and 1974 he added another seventeen test caps to his collection. He was an outstanding performer in Great Britain's World Cup-winning squad in France in 1972 and became a British Lion when he toured Australasia in 1974, playing seventeen games, including all six tests. In this purple period in his career, Paul Charlton was recognised as the world's top full-back. His attacking play was simply stunning and the game had never seen a full-back, who scored tries in such a torrent. Paul was more than an attacking machine, however, for he was a magnificent defender too. His speed enabled him to cut down even the quickest wingers and he had that unteachable knack of being able to shepherd ball-carriers to where he wanted them.

Paul returned to Workington Town in 1975 as player-coach on a free transfer, guiding them to promotion in his first season back at Derwent Park. He played the best part of another six seasons for them, captaining them to four consecutive Lancashire Cup finals (1976-79). The 16-13 victory over Wigan at Warrington in the final of 1977 was undoubtedly one of the club's greatest days. By the time he played his last game for Town at Widnes on 28 December 1980, he had rattled up 419 appearances (110 tries, 77 goals) – a club record which remains unbroken. A brief spell with Blackpool Borough brought his senior career to an end in 1981. Remarkably, though, he was still turning out for Carlisle 'A' team in 1992, when he had turned fifty.

Paul Charlton was one of the genuine giants of Rugby League. Only six men in the entire history of the sport have played more first-class games than Paul's 727 in a career which lasted for 20 years and certainly no full-back has come anywhere near matching his tally of 223 tries. Unless the game changes, no full-back ever will.

James Clampitt
Forward

First-class debut
17 October 1903,
Millom v. South Shields (home)
Last game
12 March 1921, Broughton Rangers v.
Rochdale Hornets (home) Cup
Cumberland debut
7 October 1905 v. Lancashire at Wigan
Cumberland caps
23, 1905-20
England caps
6
Test caps
2
Clubs
Millom, Broughton Rangers

'Clampitt is a capital forward. He is not one of the fancy type of scrummagers but goes in for the fair and honest work in the pack, and yet is always seen to advantage when loose play is necessary. On defence he is a sure tackler. A typical Cumbrian in that he enjoys robust, but perfectly fair forward play, and is perhaps seen to best advantage when fortune favours his opponents. This season he was appointed captain of the Broughton team, a position he is eminently qualified for. He possesses the respect and confidence of his playing colleagues and club officials, for Clampitt is one of those players who has never given any trouble either on or off the field.'

That was 'Observer's' pen picture of James Leslie Clampitt in the *Northern Union News* in April 1911. Jim Clampitt was unquestionably one of the pre-eminent forwards of the pre-First World War era. He was not particularly big at 5ft 9in and around 13st 4lbs, but he was extremely strong, hardworking and durable and he was a regular choice in the international arena.

Jim came from Millom and made his debut for his hometown club against South Shields in 1903, when the clubs both participated in the Northern Rugby League's Second Division. He made 71 appearances (four tries) for them before joining Broughton Rangers,

for whom he made his debut on 15 September 1906, scoring a try in a 17-26 defeat at Halifax.

Jim had already been capped by Cumberland while at Millom and had one of the most distinguished county careers on record. He played 23 times for Cumberland, representing them in every peacetime season between 1905 and 1920, was in the teams which defeated the first New Zealanders at Workington in 1908 and the first Australians at Carlisle in 1909 and gained County Championship winners' medals in 1907/08 and 1911/12.

He made his England debut on 4 December 1909 at Wakefield, scoring a try in a 19-13 win over Wales. He won further caps against Wales in 1911, 1912, 1913 and 1914, scoring twice in the 40-16 victory in 1913 at Plymouth. In 1911 he was in the England team which lost 11-6 to Australia at Fulham and he was also on the losing team for the Northern Rugby League against the Kangaroos at Wigan. Jim won his first test cap against Australia at Newcastle on 8 November 1911 and another against New Zealand at Auckland in 1914. As a member of the 1914 Lions, he played in eleven of the nineteen tour fixtures, scoring two tries.

At club level Jim's greatest achievement was to lead Broughton Rangers to victory over Wigan in the 1911 Challenge Cup final. He made around 260 peacetime appearances for Rangers, running in 32 tries.

Richard Clampitt
Forward

First-class debut
1 October 1904, Millom v. Keighley (away)
Last game
10 April 1920,
Broughton Rangers v. Oldham (home)
Cumberland debut
4 February 1909, v. Australians at Carlisle
Cumberland caps
9, 1909-19
Clubs
Millom, Broughton Rangers

Dick Clampitt was the younger brother of Jim Clampitt. While his career at club level followed Jim's almost exactly, Dick did not reach international status. Nonetheless, he was a rattling good forward, proficient in the basics of scrummaging, tackling and dribbling and tough as old boots. At 5ft 10in, he was a little taller than Jim but weighed a few pounds less.

Dick joined his brother in the Millom pack in 1904 and played a dozen games for the Salthouse club. He also dabbled in soccer at Barrow but eventually rejoined Jim at Broughton Rangers, scoring on his debut in a 17-13 home victory over Leeds on 5 September 1908. It was the first of fourteen tries he would score in over 200 games for Rangers.

Broughton Rangers were a major importer of Cumbrian players in the early part of the twentieth century and their presence significantly contributed to Rangers' successes. By 1908 they were slipping, however, and the 1909/10 season saw them fall calamitously to 22nd in the Northern Rugby League. It was therefore a colossal shock to the Northern Union world in 1911 when Broughton Rangers, with five Cumbrians in the team, reached the Challenge Cup final, having finished 18th in the league. They were regarded as sacrificial lambs for their opponents, top of the league Wigan at Salford. However, the heavens opened and reduced the pitch to a quagmire, completely nullifying Wigan's massive advantages in back power. Rangers' pack, which included three Cumbrians, destroyed Wigan's in loose play and Dick took a winner's medal from Broughton's 4-0 victory. It was certainly the

crowning moment of Dick Clampitt's career when he accepted the medal from the Earl of Derby.

Similarly vile conditions prevailed when Dick made his county debut against the Australians at Devonshire Park, Carlisle on 4 February 1909 and it was one of the roughest games anyone had ever seen, the referee being abjectly weak. Dick played one of the games of his life as the Kangaroos were beaten 11-2. In 1911/12 he gained his only County Championship winner's medal, Cumberland clinching the title 16-13 against Yorkshire on his old stamping ground at Millom, having already walloped Lancashire 28-7 at Warrington. He could not, however, prevent Cumberland going down 5-2 to the Kangaroos at Maryport on 22 November 1911.

In the last peacetime season, 1914/15, Dick appeared in all of Broughton's 34 fixtures and was still appearing for Rangers in 1919/20. He made his ninth and final appearance for Cumberland in a 25-9 loss to Yorkshire at Hunslet on 22 October 1919, having lost, like most of his contemporaries, some of his best years to the First World War.

Douglas Clark

Loose-forward

First-class debut
25 September 1909,
Huddersfield v. Hull KR (away)
Last game
22 January 1930,
Cumberland v. Yorkshire at Huddersfield
Cumberland debut
25 October 1910, v. Yorkshire at Dewsbury
Cumberland caps
31, 1910-30
England caps
7
Test caps
11
Club
Huddersfield

It was about 1940 in Huddersfield. The police inspector followed Jennie Clark into the front room where a massively muscled, middle-aged man was dangling a young man upside-down by his leg. He was only using one arm. 'Don't worry about them. It's only Douglas and the lodger', said Jennie. 'This sort of thing is always going off in this house'. It was a business call of sorts. The inspector had come to arrange for the older man to give some of his constables lessons in wrestling holds. He could not believe how strong this chap was. Nor could most other people.

This was Douglas Clark. The lodger was Stanley Pepperell, a half-back, who played for Huddersfield, Cumberland and England. Douglas returned Stanley to earth just missing the piano in doing so.

Douglas Clark came from Ellenborough, where he was born in 1891. He was a legend in two hemispheres. People who witnessed him in action on the rugby field or wrestling, swore he was the strongest man on the planet. He had won many wrestling prizes at Lakeland sports, including the Grasmere Cup in 1922 and 1924. He had been champion wrestler of the British Army during the First World War and in the 1930s he had become a champion 'all-in' wrestler, twice fighting in Australia. There were

tales of him breaking a belligerent bull's neck in Patterdale. He had won the Military Medal, been blown up at Passchendaele and twice gassed. As Cumbrian legends go, he was the genuine article.

It was as a Rugby League forward, however, that Douglas Clark earned his greatest fame. He played his junior rugby with Brookland Rovers and joined Huddersfield in 1909 for a fee of £30. His first-team debut, at Hull KR on 25 September 1909, ended in a 3-14 defeat. By the time he played his 485th and final game for Huddersfield twenty years later, both he and his team had secured undying fame.

Huddersfield, under the leadership of Harold Wagstaff ('The Prince of Centres'), established themselves as 'The Team of All the Talents', whilst Douglas developed a reputation as one of the finest loose-forwards the game has ever seen. Despite his enormous strength, Clark was renowned for his clean, almost chivalrous, conduct on the field. His power helped him to claim 99 tries for the Fartowners, and his scores in representative games pushed his tally well over the century, a remarkable feat for a forward in those early times. Yet he was not simply a powerhouse. He played the game intelligently, was adept at dribbling, a good tackler and capable of opening out play with his passing. It helped that he was a tee-totaller, non-smoker and a prototype fitness fanatic.

When Clark joined Huddersfield they had never won a trophy nor appeared in a final of

any description since entering the Northern Union. Two months after his debut things began to change. On 27 November 1909 at Headingley, 22,000 saw Douglas (second from right in photograph) in the Huddersfield pack that helped to rout Batley 22-0 in the Yorkshire Cup final. He would go on to earn seven winner's medals for the Yorkshire Cup and half a dozen winner's medals for the Yorkshire League Championship. He would be a member of Challenge Cup-winning sides in 1913, 1915 and 1920 and he played in five Championship finals, three of which ended in victories (1912, 1913 and 1915). Remarkably he scored tries in three Championship finals, excelling himself in 1913 when he scored a unique forward's hat-trick in a 29-2 defeat of Wigan at Wakefield.

Undoubtedly Huddersfield's greatest season was 1914/15 when they lifted all four cups, emulating Hunslet's feat of 1907/08. They were so dominant that even the three finals they contested were practically walkovers. Douglas was a major figure as Hull were beaten 31-0 in the Yorkshire Cup final, St Helens 37-3 in the Challenge Cup final and Leeds 35-2 in the Championship final, the Cumbrian scoring a try in the latter.

That Douglas Clark was one of the pre-eminent players of his times is reflected in his numerous representative selections. His test career spanned nine years (1911-20), while he played his last international as late as 7 February 1925, appropriately enough at Workington. He scored a smart try as England pipped Wales 27-22. He toured Australasia as a Lion in 1914 and 1920, scoring the winning try in his last test appearance, when New Zealand were beaten 11-10 at Wellington on 14 August 1920. His most memorable test, however, was unquestionably the epic Rorke's Drift Test of 4 July 1914 when Britain won the Ashes with a 14-6 victory over Australia at Sydney, despite being reduced to ten men for part of the game. Douglas was one of the British casualties, breaking a thumb in the first half and then dislocating his collar-bone on the hour, shedding tears of frustration at being forcibly led off the pitch.

Perhaps even more remarkable than his international longevity was his service to Cumberland County. Douglas made his county debut as a nineteen year old against Yorkshire in 1910. His last appearance, also against Yorkshire, was on his home ground, Fartown, in January, 1930, a few months before his thirty-ninth birthday. His 31 Cumberland caps have only been bettered by Joe Oliver. Douglas had been elevated to the captaincy in 1923 and had in fact come out of retirement to represent Cumberland for all three county fixtures in 1929/30.

Geoff Clark

Winger, centre

First-class debut
24 February 1945,
Dewsbury v. Wakefield Trinity (home)
Last game
29 September 1951,
Dewsbury v. Salford (home)
Cumberland debut
26 January 1946, v. Lancashire at
Workington
Cumberland caps
7, 1946-50
England caps
2
Club
Dewsbury

'D'Artagnan' wrote in *Rugby League Review* in 1952 that, 'Geoff Clark was, perhaps, not in the category of the brilliant, but he was that eminently useful type without which no team is complete – a sound, competent footballer and a good club man. His steady defence has served Dewsbury well on many an occasion, while his forceful running on the attack has brought plenty of tries for himself and his team-mates'.

Geoff was a native of Aspatria, who had signed for Dewsbury while serving in the RAF. His debut, under the alias 'Thomas', came in a 12-10 victory over Wakefield Trinity at Crown Flatt in February 1945. He was in the company of stars as Dewsbury were still utilising many guest players under wartime regulations. Gus Risman, Bert Day and George Curran were still on loan from Salford and the great Vic Hey had formally transferred from Leeds, while Dewsbury had their own resident stars in Jim Ledgard, Harry Hammond and Harry Royal. He had joined a good team and it remained a major challenger for honours even when the guests left in 1945/46.

In his first full season Geoff scored fifteen tries for Dewsbury, including his first hat-trick against Rochdale Hornets, and he played in the Yorkshire Cup semi-final when Dewsbury lost 2-7 at home to Bradford. Geoff was primarily a winger but in 1946/47 he was moved to centre as Dewsbury won the Yorkshire League Championship and reached the Championship final. At Maine Road they lost 4-13 to Wigan but Geoff was the outstanding figure with a magnificent display of tackling and penetrative running.

Dewsbury failed to win any more trophies in Geoff's time with them, although they fell at the semi-final hurdle in the Yorkshire Cup at home to Huddersfield in 1949. Geoff went close to equalling Dai Thomas's club record of eight tries in a match set in 1907, when he bagged seven in a 53-2 first-round Yorkshire Cup massacre of Yorkshire Amateurs on 13 September 1947. In 178 appearances for Dewsbury (111 on the wing, 61 at centre, five at full-back and one at stand-off) he totalled 71 tries but was forced to retire early from the game after a succession of shoulder injuries.

In seven appearances for Cumberland he claimed five tries. His first two caps were won as a centre, the remainder as a left-winger. He was a member of the team that won the County Championship in 1948/49 and had the unusual experience of playing opposite his fellow Dewsbury winger Roy Pollard when Cumberland met Yorkshire at Hull on 26 September 1949. He was the match-winner at Whitehaven in 1950 scoring both tries in a 10-5 defeat of Yorkshire. Geoff also attained international status, appearing for England against Other Nationalities in 1949 at Workington and 1951 at Wigan.

Tony Colloby
Centre, winger

First-class debut
19 August 1961,
Whitehaven v. Hunslet (away)
Last game
6 September 1974,
Barrow v. Doncaster (home)
Cumberland debut
25 September 1963, v. Yorkshire at
Wakefield
Cumberland caps
20, 1963-73
Clubs
Whitehaven, Workington Town, Blackpool
Borough, Salford, Barrow

Strong-running, elusive and opportunistic, Tony Colloby was a product of Kendal RU club. He joined Whitehaven in 1961 and developed into a talented centre who also gave good service as a wingman. In his second game for Whitehaven, he decided the issue by scoring both tries in a 6-4 win against Bramley, then scored twelve points in his next home game against York. His first season ended gloriously when he set a new club record by bagging five tries in a 34-4 home rout of Liverpool City on 10 March 1962.

His debut season saw him top Whitehaven's try-scorers with 21 in 20 games. He topped the lists again in 1962/63 with another 20. He scored 50 tries and ten goals for Whitehaven in 81 appearances before decamping to Workington in 1964. Town still had some of their great players from the 1950s but won nothing in the four years Tony was with them. He scored 33 tries and four goals for Workington in 93 appearances.

He then moved south to Blackpool Borough in 1968, scoring twice on his debut against Huyton. Blackpool seemed to be a last resting place for the greats of the game. Tony partnered Billy Boston on his Blackpool debut on Boxing Day 1969, the other three-quarters being Ray Ashby and John Stopford, both former Great Britain stars. Tony topped the try-scorers with 17 in 1968/69 and 13 in 1969/70.

Having rattled up 35 tries and 26 goals in 76 games for Borough, he transferred to Salford in 1970. There he joined a star-studded side, containing such luminaries as Paul Charlton, Chris Hesketh, Colin Dixon, Maurice Richards and David Watkins and he thrived. At last he had a chance to win honours and 1972/73 brought some. Salford won the Lancashire Cup beating Swinton 25-11 in the final and Tony received a winner's medal, despite missing the final. He had scored five tries in the first two rounds and played in the semi against Wigan. Later in the season he played in the Players Trophy final, although Salford lost 7-12 to Leeds at Fartown. He played 43 games that season, mostly on the wing, claiming 22 tries, including two against the 1970 New Zealand World Cup side.

In 89 games for Salford he scored 41 tries and three goals. His final stop was for a year at Barrow in 1973, where he made sixteen appearances (two tries, four goals), all at centre.

With twenty caps, Tony Colloby was one of Cumberland's most decorated players in a county career which stretched from 1963 to 1973, hardly missing a game. He was a try-scorer on his debut against Yorkshire in a 15-13 win at Wakefield and took a County Championship winner's medal when Lancashire were beaten 13-8 at Whitehaven. Other winners' medals followed in 1965 and 1966. Remarkably, he represented Cumberland while playing for each of his five professional clubs.

Gordon Cottier

Centre, loose-forward, second row, prop

First-class debut
18 February 1968,
Whitehaven v. Blackpool Borough (away)
Last game
12 March 1986,
Workington Town v. Carlisle (away)
Cumberland debut
24 October 1973, v. Australians at
Whitehaven
Cumbria caps
6, 1973-81
Clubs
Whitehaven, Barrow (loan), Workington
Town

Gordon Cottier's Rugby League career displayed fortitude and resilience of the highest order, while his durability, enthusiasm and versatility have rarely been emulated.

Gordon was signed by Whitehaven, his hometown club, from the Moresby Rugby Union club in 1967. He made his debut at right centre in a 10-10 draw at Blackpool Borough in February 1968, scoring a try, the first of only 36 he would claim for the club in 340 appearances. He also landed four goals, two of which were dropped. For five years Gordon struggled to establish a permanent place in the team but once he had moved to loose-forward he did not look back.

In 1972/73 he was a key member of the team which won First Division status for Whitehaven, when the decision to abandon a single league was taken. In 1974/75 he scored the opening try in Whitehaven's John Player Trophy semi-final against Bradford Northern at the Recreation Ground but Northern ran out 18-6 winners. That was the closest Gordon got to appearing in a major final.

In 1975/76 Gordon did not miss any of Whitehaven's thirty fixtures and in the subsequent two seasons he was missing for only two games out of 62. It came as a huge blow then

when doctors told him to retire because of a heart problem. He had already played ten years and 233 games for Whitehaven, a lot more than most players could expect.

He missed the 1978/79 and 1979/80 seasons but returned at open-side prop on 7 September 1980 in a 10-23 defeat at Hunslet. He played 26 games that season as Whitehaven won promotion. They were relegated straightaway but in 1982/83 Gordon led them back to Division One, only for the process to be repeated but for a man with a heart condition it was pretty amazing.

He continued to bolster the Whitehaven pack until 28 April 1985, when he made his last appearance in a 26-28 defeat at Sheffield Eagles. Gordon had played for 'Haven as a centre (30 times), loose-forward (84), second-row (137), blind-side prop (45) and open-side prop (23) and made 21 substitute appearances. In 1972 he had made five appearances on loan with Barrow and in a similar arrangement had turned out six times for Workington in 1986. He finished his career with Town in 1985/86, scoring two tries in nine games.

A skilful and creative player, Gordon was first capped by Cumbria at loose-forward against the 1973 Australian tourists at Whitehaven, the Kangaroos winning 28-2. He went on to win six caps, scoring one try against Yorkshire at York in 1977. His county career fittingly came to a climax in 1981, when Lancashire were beaten 27-15 at Wigan and Yorkshire 20-10 at Whitehaven to give Cumbria the title and Gordon a well-deserved winner's medal.

Jack Coulson
Winger, centre

First-class debut
16 April 1924, Hunslet v. Wigan (away)
Last game
26 November 1932, Halifax v. Wigan (away)
Cumberland debut
29 October 1925, v. Yorkshire at
Huddersfield
Cumberland caps
18, 1925-32
Clubs
Hunslet, Halifax

John, usually known as Jack, Coulson went from Millom to Hunslet in 1924, where he became one of the most consistent three-quarters in the game for almost a decade. He was equally good at centre, in which position he played 117 games for Hunslet, and on the wing, where he made 140 appearances. He also turned out at stand-off on sixteen occasions.

In his first full season at Parkside he topped the try-scorers with sixteen, including a hat-trick against Halifax in only his fifth senior appearance. He was again top in 1925/26 with seventeen but his most prolific season was 1929/30 when he ran over for 22 tries, including one in a stunning 18-3 defeat of the Australians on Christmas Day. It was also that season, when he won his first medal, figuring at right centre in Hunslet's 7-13 Yorkshire Cup final defeat by Hull KR at Headingley.

Two years later there was another runners-up medal for him in the Yorkshire Cup, when 27,800 saw Huddersfield pip Hunslet 4-2 at Headingley, Jack again being in the centre. Hunslet reached the Championship semi-final, once more losing to Huddersfield, 9-12 at Fartown, although Jack missed the game. He did, however, gain a Yorkshire League Championship-winner's medal.

Jack played his 273rd and last game for Hunslet on 26 September 1932, in a 21-3 reverse at St Helens, having amassed 106 tries as a Parksider. He was transferred to Halifax but retired after playing only six matches, scoring a solitary try against Barrow on 5 November 1932.

At 5ft 9in and 11st, Jack Coulson was a bit on the small side for centre but compensated for a lack of poundage with skill, enthusiasm and good positioning, and his speed as a winger was a bonus for the inside position.

Cumberland preferred to use Jack on the wings. Of his eighteen caps only three were won as a centre, all in the 1929/30 campaign, when the Australians, at Workington, and Glamorgan & Monmouth, at Cardiff, were both vanquished. He scored two tries on his debut in a shock 31-13 triumph over Yorkshire at Huddersfield in 1925. In 1927/28 he received a County Championship-winner's medal after Cumberland's victories over Lancashire at Whitehaven (27-2), Glamorgan & Monmouth at Pontypridd (18-12) and Yorkshire at Wakefield (11-5).

In 1932/33, his last season in the game, he wrote his name in the history books and earned a second County Championship-winner's medal. On 1 October 1932, Cumberland annihilated a strong Yorkshire team 39-10 at Whitehaven. Billy Holding kicked six goals and Cumberland collected nine tries. Jack was in devastating finishing form on the right wing to claim four – a record which no Cumbrian has ever emulated in a county match. The title was sealed two weeks later when Lancashire were beaten 9-3 at Barrow.

Paddy Dalton

Second-row, loose-forward

First-class debut
1 November 1930,
Salford v. Wigan Highfield (away)
Last game
18 May 1940,
Salford v. Broughton Rangers (away)
Cumberland debut
28 October 1933, v. Lancashire at Workington
Cumberland caps
13, 1933-38
England caps
5
Club
Salford

Salford produced one of the finest teams in Rugby League history in the 1930s under manager Lance Todd and captain Gus Risman. At the heart of a wonderfully virile and constructive pack was Patrick Dalton from Harrington, a second-row forward of fine pace and, according to one critic, 'a true Cumbrian in defence'. He was good on attack too, a pen picture in 1939 declaring, 'Salford folk say that Dalton throws out to his backs more telling passes than any other forward in the game'.

Paddy made his debut in unusual circumstances in 1930 in a game at Wigan Highfield, which was abandoned at half-time with Salford leading 6-2. He went on to play 291 games for Salford, scoring 58 tries over the next ten years.

In his first full season he earned a Lancashire Cup-winner's medal, although he did not play in the final. He did appear in Salford's next four Lancashire Cup finals, however, all against Wigan, in 1934, 1935, 1936 and 1938, all of which were won, except the last. Salford were so dominant that they won the Lancashire League Championship in 1932/33, 1933/34, 1934/35, 1936/37 and 1938/39, adding another five medals to Paddy's cabinet.

Salford appeared in four Championship finals in Paddy's time at The Willows. He missed the first two but played in victories over Warrington in 1937 and Castleford in

1939, the latter before a British record crowd of 69,504 at Maine Road. In 1938 he played in the Wembley final victory over Barrow, being one of the better performers in a poor game. He was back at Wembley in 1939, suffering from the after-effects of 'flu, as Salford went down to Halifax.

Although he was normally a second-rower, most of his representative honours were won at loose-forward. His Cumberland career kicked off in 1933 at a wet and stormy Workington, when Lancashire were beaten 10-0. This was the first time the legendary back-row of Martin Hodgson, Alec Troup and Paddy Dalton took the field together. The County Championship was won, when Paddy was among the scorers in a 15-11 victory over Yorkshire at Dewsbury, and his third appearance for Cumberland saw a defeat for the Australians at Whitehaven. Paddy gained a second County Championship-winner's medal in 1934/35.

He twice represented Rugby League XIIIs in victories over France, at Warrington in 1934 and at Leeds in 1935. On 13 January 1934, he won his first England cap against Australia at Gateshead and was one of four Cumbrians in the team which won 19-14. Three months later he played in England's first international against France in Paris, a 32-21 victory. It was 84 degrees in the shade and the England players got £5 winning pay. Paddy won five England caps but surprisingly never won test recognition.

First-class debut*
10 January 1903,
Cumberland v. Lancashire at Millom
Last game
25 December 1911,
Oldham v. Hull KR (home)
Cumberland caps
18, 1903-11
Club
Oldham

*Billy Dixon's first class club debut was on 5
September 1903, for Oldham v. Hull (home)

Born and bred in Maryport, Billy Dixon had
already played his first game for Cumberland
before he joined Oldham in 1903. At the
time he was a half-back, but eight highly
successful seasons at Watersheddings saw him
fill all the back positions except full-back.

Billy was a little bull of a man. Just 5ft 6in
tall, he weighed 13st, which was exceptionally
heavy for a back in those times, particularly
for one so short. He was not very quick but he
was strong, direct and determined. He took a
lot of stopping.

He must have felt at home at Oldham for
there were three other Cumbrians in the side
when he made his debut – Frank Spottiswoode,
Joe Ferguson and Joe Owens. Billy quickly
settled at stand-off and in his second season
Oldham won the First Division Championship
to start his medal collection. By 1906/07, the
first season of thirteen-a-side, Billy had moved
via scrum-half to centre as Oldham enjoyed a
fabulous campaign, which ended in the anti-
climax of defeat in both the Challenge Cup
final against Warrington and in the inaugural
Championship final against Halifax.

The following season brought him another
Championship runners-up medal but also
winners' medals for the Lancashire Cup, when
Broughton Rangers were overcome 16-9 at
Rochdale, and for the Lancashire League.
Billy was also in the Oldham team that beat
the New Zealanders 8-7.

In 1908/09 he was back at half-back, when
Oldham lost to Wigan in both the Lancashire
Cup final and the Championship final. The
fact that he was so versatile helped enor-
mously for this Oldham team was filled with
star backs from all corners of the Rugby
League world – but there was always a place
for Billy.

Oldham won the Lancashire League and
the Championship in 1909/10, Billy scoring a
try in the final when revenge was gained on
Wigan 13-7 at Broughton. His last full season,
1910/11, brought more success with winners'
medals for the Lancashire Cup, Swinton being
beaten 4-3 in the final, and retention of the
Championship, Wigan again the victims by
20-7. Billy played on the wing in both finals.

Billy gave good service to Cumberland. On
his debut at Millom against Lancashire he was
one of five Maryport representatives, at a time
when many players from junior clubs could
still win caps and the game was played fifteen-
a-side. By the time he finished his county
career, also at Millom against Yorkshire in
1911, the game was much changed, faster and
thirteen-a-side. Billy played in County
Championship winning sides in 1907/08 and
1911/12 and in teams that shared the title in
1905/06 and 1909/10. His biggest thrill,
however, was scoring the first try from a
headlong rush to the corner in Cumberland's
victory over the New Zealanders at
Workington in 1908.

First-class debut
11 April 1953, Hull v. Halifax (home)
Last game
18 February 1967,
York v. Wakefield Trinity (home)
Cumberland debut
5 October 1955, v. Yorkshire at Bradford
Cumberland caps
10, 1955-63
England caps
1
Test caps
1
Clubs
Hull, Leeds, York

Bill Drake was Jim Drake's twin brother and younger by about ten minutes. The two looked and played completely differently. Bill was 6ft 1.5in – two and a half inches taller than Jim, and weighed half a stone less at 14st 7lbs. Born in 1931 in Workington, the pair also had a younger brother Joe, who played professionally for York.

Bill originally played on the wing, where he made his debut for Hull in a 9-12 home defeat by Halifax in 1953, partnered by the great Roy Francis. Two days later Bill scored two tries in a 31-12 beating of Castleford, the first of 101 he would score for Hull. By 1955, his days in the backs were numbered and his transformation into a top-class second-rower had taken place. He had good pace, excellent handling skills and an ability to make play constructively. He was also a handy goal-kicker, landing 53 for Hull.

Cumberland first recognised his ability in 1955, when they played him at loose-forward against Yorkshire at Odsal. His career for the county would span eight years. Oddly, he would play five games for Cumberland against Yorkshire in five positions – loose-forward, centre, second-row, open-side prop and blind-side prop. International recognition came late, however. Although a tour trialist in

1958, it was not until 1962 that he was capped, by which time he was a prop. With fellow Cumbrians Dick Huddart and Brian Edgar, he formed half of England's pack in an 18-6 victory over France at Headingley on 17 November. A fortnight later he won his solitary test cap at Perpignan, when France beat Great Britain 17-12.

In 1955 Bill appeared in his first major final for Hull, when they drew a torrid Yorkshire Cup final with Halifax at Headingley, losing the replay 0-7 at Bradford. He was much happier six months later, on 12 May 1956, when he shared in Hull's 10-9 revenge win over Halifax in the Championship final at Maine Road. A year later he felt the pain of defeat in a Championship final, when Oldham beat his team 15-14 at Odsal. Hull reached a third consecutive Championship final in 1958, beating Workington Town but Bill was missing through injury, a fate which also befell him when Hull went down to Wakefield in the 1960 Challenge Cup final. He had, however, appeared at Wembley the previous year in Hull's defeat by Wigan.

After 293 games for Hull, Bill moved to Leeds in 1963, making 32 appearances as a Loiner, kicking three goals on his debut against Widnes, and appearing in another Yorkshire Cup final in 1964 against Wakefield. A transfer to York in 1965 saw him reverting from prop to second-row for most of the 48 games he played for the club, before ending his career in 1967.

Jim Drake
Prop-forward

First-class debut
26 March 1951,
Hull v. Featherstone Rovers (home)
Last game
6 February 1965,
Hull KR v. Batley (home) Cup
Cumberland debut
19 September 1956, v. Yorkshire at
Whitehaven
Cumberland caps
6, 1956-62
Test caps
1
Clubs
Hull, Hull KR

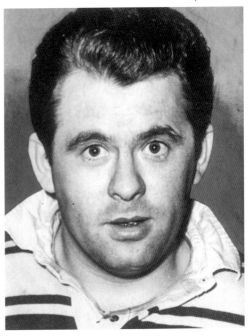

'I never played in any game with Jim Drake without some kind of set to, he was such a dirty bastard. You had to watch him like a hawk.' Those were the words of international prop Terry Clawson, no shrinking violet himself, in his autobiography in 2000. He later added the observation that 'off the field he was a great bloke!'

There is no doubt that Workington-born Jim Drake was one of the toughest of the tough in an era marked by both brilliant individualism and physical robustness, the 1950s and 1960s. Belligerence could have been his middle name. Yet he started out as a full-back with York amateur club Heworth. Rheumatic fever put him out of the game for a year, his future in the game was threatened and his weight ballooned.

Hull signed him and he began his career in a 10-4 home win over Featherstone in 1951, still playing at full-back. Moving through loose-forward and second-row, Jim ultimately established himself as first-choice prop in one of the game's most potent ever packs in 1956. He made his county debut the same year, scoring a try in Cumberland's 15-14 win over Yorkshire at Whitehaven, with John McKeown landing a last-minute match-winning penalty. Jim's county career was badly affected by injuries, however.

His representative career was similarly affected. In 1958, at the height of his powers, he was selected for the Great Britain tour of Australasia but had to withdraw because of an injured knee. He was replaced by Abe Terry

(St Helens). He had to wait until 1960 for his solitary test cap, when he and club colleague Tommy Harris were in Britain's front row in an 18-20 defeat by France at Toulouse.

Hull played in many finals during Jim's time at The Boulevard, but injuries caused him to miss several. He did earn Championship-winners' medals in 1955/56 and 1957/58 but missed both finals. In between, he played in the Championship final of 1957 only to finish on the losing side to Oldham. In 1959 he played at Wembley but then missed the Cup final the following year, Hull losing heavily on both occasions. In 1959 he also received a runners-up medal in the Yorkshire Cup.

After playing 243 games (38 tries, 1 goal) for Hull, he crossed the city to Hull KR, for whom he went on to play 64 games (3 tries) between 1961 and 1965. With Rovers he appeared in three consecutive losing Challenge Cup semi-finals and the Yorkshire Cup final of 1962, when Hunslet – with broken bones to skipper Harry Poole and centre Mike Blackmore – beat them 12-2. His bad luck in major finals at last broke in 1962, when he figured in the Robins' 13-10 victory over Huddersfield at Headingley in the newly instituted Eastern Division Championship final.

BRADFORD'S CUMBRIAN CRACK.

First-class debut
19 November 1898,
Cumberland v. Cheshire at Runcorn
First class club debut
2 September 1899, Millom v. Widnes (away)
Cumberland caps
20, 1898-1910
Yorkshire caps
3, 1902
England caps
1

Clubs
Millom, Bradford, Hunslet, Bradford Northern

Born in Millom, Bill Eagers graduated through the Millom Rangers and Haverigg teams to the senior Millom XV by the time he was sixteen. He forged a formidable reputation as a full-back, thoroughly adept in tackling, goal-kicking and fielding the ball. He would, however, go on to fame as a centre with two of Yorkshire's most famous clubs, taking part in several historic 'firsts'.

In 1900/01 he joined Bradford, aristocrats of the Northern Union, who retained the Yorkshire Senior Competition Championship. It was the first of many medals for Bill, who elected to play for Yorkshire in 1902. He had been a member of the very first Cumberland Northern Union team in 1898 and became the first Cumbrian to win 20 caps for the county. In 1903/04 Bradford won the NU First Division Championship after beating Salford 5-0 in a play-off at Halifax.

In 1905 he left Bradford, for whom he had scored 28 tries and 42 goals in 121 games, and signed for Hunslet. Hunslet became first winners of the Yorkshire Cup when they beat Halifax 13-3, ironically at Bradford. Bill repaid his old club by smashing one of the pavilion windows with a huge kick to touch!

A month later, on New Year's Day 1906,

Bill played for England in a 3-3 draw against Other Nationalities at Wigan in the last ever fifteen-a-side international.

In 1907/08 Hunslet became the first team to perform the supremely difficult feat of winning All Four Cups. Bill played in 40 of Hunslet's games that campaign, including a drawn clash with the first touring team to Britain, Baskerville's New Zealanders. Four days earlier Bill had dropped a goal in Hunslet's 17-0 Yorkshire Cup final rout of Halifax at Headingley. He dropped another crucial goal at Fartown as Hunslet beat Hull 14-0 in the Challenge Cup final. A week later, Hunslet drew their Championship final against Oldham at Salford. The replay, however, at Wakefield, saw Bill's side create history with a 12-2 victory.

In 1908/09 Bill played in another Yorkshire Cup final, which Hunslet lost 5-9 to Halifax, and in an 11-12 loss to the first Kangaroos. He left Hunslet having made 131 appearances (37 tries, 16 goals), returning to Bradford Northern, the club that had succeeded his old club. Northern were a shadow of the old Bradford and Bill stayed for a solitary season, playing 14 games (2 tries, 10 goals) before returning to Hunslet for the 1910/11 season – his last. Like Bradford, Hunslet were in rapid decline and Bill played only 14 more games for them (6 goals). He did, however, make a final appearance in an injury crisis in 1914.

Fighting in German East Africa in the First World War, Bill was severely wounded. Hunslet rallied to his assistance by playing a testimonial match for him in 1921.

First-class debut
9 April 1955,
Workington Town v. Huddersfield (away)
Last game
28 October 1967,
Workington Town v. Salford (home)
Cumberland debut
14 September 1960,
v. Yorkshire at Whitehaven
Cumberland caps
13, 1960-67
England caps
1
Test caps
11
Club
Workington Town

If the wisest men in the game's history were assembled and asked to select the three best forwards to have been produced by Cumberland in the century or more since the Northern Union was formed, it is a safe bet that they would perm any three from the following four: Duggie Clark, Joe Ferguson, Martin Hodgson and, most recently, Brian Edgar.

Brian Edgar was certainly the complete forward. He had everything, except perhaps a malicious streak. He was massive, ending his career at over 16st, and as strong as a bull but he also had a delicious side-step. He had a steam-piston of a hand-off, excellent handling skills, would tackle for eighty minutes and was mobile enough to register 99 career tries. His temper was amazing for a player who was so often in the heat of the most torrid battles, never coming under the referee's ban in over 400 matches.

Born in Great Broughton in 1936, Brian attended Cockermouth Grammar School and developed into a superb Rugby Union forward, playing for England Schools, Workington Zebras and Cumberland. In 1955 Tom Mitchell lured him away from union, however, to sign for Workington Town, his only professional club. His debut, in the second-row alongside Johnny Mudge, just a week or so after his nineteenth birthday was at Fartown, where Workington were annihilated

44-13 by Huddersfield. Two days later Town used him on the left wing at Hull KR and he scored three tries playing outside Eppie Gibson, while the other centre, Tony Paskins, collected Town's remaining four tries and five goals in a 31-8 success.

Workington had already fought their way into the Challenge Cup final and Brian was not really expecting to figure at Wembley. At the last minute it was decided that he would play in the final, regular second-rower Norm Herbert being declared unfit. The final against Barrow on 30 April 1955 constituted Brian's sixth first-team game. Of course, it was memorable but for the wrong reasons. The first hour was a dreary, try-less affair before Barrow took full control to run out winners by 21-12. Brian had to play the last half-hour on the left wing in a positional reshuffle caused by injury to scrum-half Sol Roper. It is probable that up to 1955, at least, Brian was the youngest forward to have played at Wembley.

He was back at Wembley in 1958 when Workington went 22 games without defeat and appeared set to accomplish the league and cup double. That Town reached

Wembley at all was due to Brian Edgar's try in the first round which beat Leigh 3-0 at Derwent Park, while he was also a try-scorer in a third round 11-0 defeat of Warrington. At Wembley against Wigan, Brian made the game's first try when he cut through majestically, baffled two men and sent Ike Southward haring thirty yards to the line. The newspaper critics almost unanimously made Brian the best forward on the field in the first half. The second half, however, was a nightmare. Brian spent most of the half concussed and injuries to Andy Key and Harry Archer ensured that Wigan won 13-9.

The following week, Town met Hull at Odsal in the Championship final. Again Brian conjured an early try for Southward but again injury, this time to Cec Thompson, who missed the last 55 minutes, decided the issue and Town went down 20-3.

Although the domestic season had ended badly for Brian and Town, 1958 was the year that Brian established himself as one of the world's best forwards. In March he had played

in a tour trial at Swinton, had played well but had been left out of the Lions touring party. He was drafted in, however, when fellow Cumbrian Sid Little withdrew.

The tour was a triumph for Britain, who won the Ashes. Brian made his test debut in the first test at Sydney that was lost, but he excelled, at prop, in a 32-15 victory over New Zealand at Auckland. He played in sixteen tour fixtures and scored six tries. Four years later he toured again, this time playing in all three Ashes tests, the first two ending in victories. His second-row partnership with Dick Huddart was absolutely devastating and is still revered in Australia as one of the most outstanding ever seen in that country. He played eleven games (five tries) on the 1962 tour.

Brian made history in 1966, when he joined Leeds' great pre-war Welshman Joe Thompson as the only forwards to have made three Lions tours. When the Lions skipper Harry Poole was injured, Brian, now at open-side prop, was made captain of Great Britain for all three Ashes tests – the crowning glory for any player. On this tour he made 14 appearances (three tries).

Strangely, Brian only played in two tests on home soil – against New Zealand in 1961 and 1965 – and he never played a test against France, although he did represent England in an 18-6 success against them at Leeds in 1962.

Perhaps even more strangely, Brian did not win a Cumberland cap until 1960, due to a combination of injuries and unavailability. Once established in the county XIII, however, he was a permanent fixture. In his thirteen games for Cumberland eight were won and one drawn, as he captained Cumberland to four County Championships in 1961/62, 1963/64, 1965/66 and 1966/67, one of the most productive periods in the county's history.

Brian played for Workington Town until 1967, his club career encompassing 384 games, 83 tries and 27 goals. In 1962 he led Town to the inaugural Western Division Championship final in which Wigan were beaten after a replay. It was his only winner's medal, scant reward for such an icon of Cumbrian Rugby League.

Joe Ferguson
Front-row forward

First-class debut
9 September 1899, Oldham v. Millom (away)
Last game
14 April 1923, Oldham v. St Helens (away)
Cumberland debut
7 October 1905, v. Lancashire at Wigan
Cumberland caps
31, 1905-22
Lancashire caps
15, 1900-05
England caps
4
Club
Oldham

'They don't make them like that any more today' is a sentiment often expressed in many walks of life. Well, they certainly don't make Rugby League forwards like Joe Ferguson any more.

Here was a man who packed down in 677 games, at a time when there were as many as 100 scrums in a match, in a period when forwards really had to pull and push for eighty minutes, as well as tackling and dribbling with no chance of a rest by being substituted. He was a man who played until he was forty-four and served only one professional club. He was also a match-winning goal-kicker with a penchant for performing best in the biggest of games, an inspiring captain and a terror to opposing packs.

Joe Ferguson came from Maryport, where he was born in 1879. His rugby career began as a fourteen-year-old full-back for Brookland Rovers reserves. By the time he was fifteen he was in the first team and by 1899, he was sought after by several of the game's top professional clubs. Halifax actually signed him on 29 April 1899 but contravened the Northern Union rules, which stipulated that 1 May was the earliest signing date. This allowed Oldham to gazump Halifax and neither Joe nor Oldham ever regretted the deal.

Joe made his first-team debut in a friendly at Morecambe, which Oldham won 29-3 on 2 September 1899. His official debut, a week later, was on his native Cumbrian soil when Oldham were victorious 13-5 at Millom.

What followed is impossible to list in any detail in a description of this length for Ferguson's career was of veritably monumental proportions. He was playing with one of the most successful clubs in the game and cups, caps and medals became his staple diet. Joe's first caps were county caps but not for his native county.

Residential qualifications enabled him to begin his representative career with Lancashire. His Lancashire debut, before a crowd of 18,000 at Rochdale on 3 November 1900, saw him land a goal in a 24-5 victory over Yorkshire. His next game, a 30-0 rout of Cheshire at Stockport, saw him boot six goals as Lancashire took the County Championship. Over five seasons Joe won 15 Lancashire caps, including three against Cumberland, and picked up three County Championship-winners' medals. Ironically, however, his last game ended in a 11-0 loss to the Cumbrians at Whitehaven on 16 January 1905.

His next county match, at Wigan on 7 October 1905, saw everything reversed. Joe was now in the Cumberland pack that held the Lancastrians to a 3-3 draw. He would go on to represent Cumberland a (then) record 31 times, helping them to win outright titles in 1907/08 and 1911/12 and shared titles in 1905/06 and 1909/10. Remarkably, he would captain the county from 1907 until 1922. Uniquely, he played against the 1907/08 New Zealanders and against the 1908/09, 1911/12 and 1921/22 Kangaroos. Joe's combined total of 46 caps for Lancashire and Cumberland is a record that will never be broken, unless county games are restored to their historic status. Incredibly he

Cumbrian greats Tom Fletcher (left) and Joe Ferguson (right) with the celebrated New Zealander George Smith.

played county football in every peacetime season from 1900 to 1922.

Joe Ferguson was not a shrinking violet. He believed in punishing defence, his teams often being quite willing to allow opponents early possession in order to knock the stuffing out of them, which allowed the backs to play havoc at a later stage. At just under 6ft and 14st 7lbs, he was a very big forward for his own era. His aggressive, rugged style and distinctive musta-chioed face were magnets for the international selectors and Joe had the distinction of repre-senting England at twelve-a-side, thirteen-a-side and fifteen-a-side, as the game experimented and changed in its formative years.

He played in the game's very first interna-tional at Wigan in 1904 (twelve-a-side) in a 3-3 draw against Other Nationalities. In 1905 in the first fifteen-a-side international he hoofed three goals in England's 26-11 win over Other Nationalities at Bradford and, after the game had settled down to thirteen-a-side, he captained England to successes over New Zealand in 1908 and Wales in 1909. He would also have been a member of the first Lions touring team in 1910 but turned down the opportunity for business reasons.

At club level with Oldham he was equally successful. He captained 'the Spindles' to victory in every competition except the Challenge Cup, although he did play in the finals of 1907 and

1912 when Oldham were defeated by Warrington and Dewsbury. He played in five consecutive Championship finals (1906/07 onwards), leading his team to victory in 1909/10 and 1910/11, when Wigan were victims on both occasions. His days at Watersheddings saw Oldham contest eight Lancashire Cup Finals (four successfully) and win four Lancashire League Championships.

Apart from being such a force in the front row of the pack, either propping or hooking, and being such a charismatic leader, Joe Ferguson was a brilliant goal-kicker. In 1904/05 and 1905/06 he was the Northern Union's leading kicker and in his career he single-footedly won numerous games for his sides. One of his greatest goals was a drop-kick from inside his own half which enabled Oldham to beat Swinton 4-3 in the Lancashire Cup final of 1910 at Broughton.

By the time his career ended, Joe had amassed 1,362 points from 582 goals and 66 tries and he had made 682 first-class appearances (five in the backs). He played his last game for Oldham in 1923, aged 44 years and 48 days, making him the oldest man to play at the top level until Jeff Grayshon broke his record in the 1990s. It was no wonder that a critic could describe Joe in 1908 as 'the prince of goal-kickers, pride of Oldham, captain of the Spindledom XIII and captain of Cumberland County.' Yet he was only scratching the surface.

Billy Fisher

Centre, loose-forward, second-row

First-class debut
6 September 1981,
Whitehaven v. Hull (home)
Last game
2 June 1996,
Whitehaven v. Wakefield Trinity (home)
Cumbria debut
20 October 1987,
v. Papua-New Guinea at Whitehaven
Cumbria caps
3, 1987-90
Club
Whitehaven

Born in Whitehaven in 1962, Billy Fisher played his whole professional career with his hometown club. He came, however, from the Rugby Union ranks, having played for the St Benedict's club and having represented Cumbria Colts. He signed for 'Haven on 20 July 1981 and made his debut six weeks later in a 3-24 home defeat by Hull. Whitehaven were in Division One when Billy started out but were relegated at the close of his debut season.

The first decade of Billy's time at the Recreation Ground was played at centre, with occasional excursions onto the wing and stand-off. At 6ft tall and 14st, Billy had the physique for the position, was powerful on the break and had a good turn of pace. His durability and resilience became a byword in West Cumbria.

In 1982/83 Billy established himself as a first-teamer and the reward for the club was promotion back to the First Division. Unfortunately, that was the nearest Billy would ever come to silverware in his career at Whitehaven. Billy registered the first of 68 tries he would amass for the club in a Lancashire Cup-tie at Carlisle on 5 September 1982.

Whitehaven were relegated after just one season in the top flight and have never since regained that eminence. Billy, however, carried on regardless. In 1986 he began a fruitful centre partnership with the former Wales RU International Bob Ackerman. 1986/87 was one of the most successful seasons in Whitehaven's modern history. They reached the third round of the Cup,

putting out Huddersfield and Wakefield Trinity and were semi-finalists in the Second Division Premiership play-offs. The three-quarter line of Norman Lofthouse (13 tries), Billy (13), Ackerman (14) and Tony Solarie (21) proved one of the most potent in the league. Billy had the bizarre experience of scoring a try in Whitehaven's record 72-6 victory over Fulham on 14 September and ten days later scoring Whitehaven's only try in a 6-74 club record defeat at Wigan.

By 1990 Billy was being played in the second-row and loose-forward, where his pace and determination were real benefits to the pack. He would go on giving his all for another six years, sometimes as captain, for Whitehaven. When he retired in 1996 he had made 371 appearances for the club, second only to John McKeown's record of 417.

Cumbria honours came late to Billy, the first of three caps being awarded for the 1987 game against the Papuans at Whitehaven, when he partnered Kevin Pape in the centres in a 22-4 victory. His second cap also brought an 18-13 victory at the Recreation Ground in a unique encounter against France. A final cap against the Australians at Workington in 1990, opposite Brad Fittler and Cliffie Lyons, was less successful as Cumbria lost 10-42.

First-class debut
12 November 1898,
Oldham v. Rochdale Hornets (away)
Last game
11 October 1913,
Cumberland v. Yorkshire at Workington
Cumberland debut
19 November 1898, v. Cheshire at Runcorn
Cumberland caps
17, 1898-1913
Lancashire caps
3, 1899
England caps (RU)
1
Clubs (professional)
Oldham, Barrow

Even before Northern Union (Rugby League) football established itself in the area in late Victorian days, Cumberland had been renowned as a fertile breeding ground for rugby forwards. It has tended to retain that reputation in the subsequent century. Exceptional backs have been less abundant.

One notable exception, however, was Tom Fletcher, a redoubtable walrus-moustached centre from Seaton, whose career stretched from pre-Northern Union times until the First World War and who was one of the trend-setters both in his native county and in the wider game.

Tom Fletcher was born in 1874 and attended Northside Council School in Seaton but began to make his name as a rugby player with another school team, Chapel Bank Rovers in Workington. From there he graduated to the senior Seaton RU Club, helping to establish them as one of the county's major powers. As a Rugby Union player Tom played for Cumberland and the North of England and on 9 January 1897, he made history by becoming the first Cumbrian back to play for England when he turned out on the wing against Wales at Newport. It was to be his only international appearance.

Later that season Cumberland reached the final of the County Championship for the first time but Tom was on the losing side as Kent beat them 12-3 at Carlisle on 10 April 1897. By this time he was a target for the big Northern Union clubs. It was hardly surprising for he must have been a nightmare for opposing centres. He was quick and unselfish. Moreover, at 5ft 10in and 13st 7lbs, he was bigger than most contemporary forwards. Even more disconcerting for opposing backs was his habit of hurdling over tacklers, a dangerous practice upon which many critics and spectators frowned.

The club that secured his services was the biggest in Lancashire, Oldham. He made his debut for them on 12 November 1898 in a 9-0 win at Rochdale Hornets to start a momentous season. 1898/99 was the first season in which Cumberland entered the Northern Union County Championship and Tom was in the centre for their inaugural game – a 4-3 loss to Cheshire at Runcorn on 19 November. He was also in the first Cumberland team to win a match a fortnight later when Lancashire were downed 13-3 at Lonsdale Park, Workington.

He continued to write his name in history at club level. Oldham finished runners-up in the Lancashire Senior Competition but when the 1899 Challenge Cup came round, there was no stopping them. Tom scored four tries in a first round 63-0 drubbing of Goole, scored another try in a quarter-final defeat of Widnes and dropped a goal in the semi-final against Leigh. The final against Hunslet was staged at Fallowfield, Manchester on 29 April 1899. Oldham triumphed 19-9 to become the first Lancashire club to lift the Challenge Cup. Tom was thought by many to have been the game's outstanding player, as he became the first Cumbrian to earn a Challenge Cup-winner's medal, arguably still the most coveted reward the game has to offer.

Oldham made him their captain for 1899/1900 and he almost took them to the Lancashire Senior Competition title only for them to be pipped by Runcorn. He did, however, earn a County Championship winner's medal. Residential qualifications entitled him to play for Lancashire and he figured in all three of their victories over Cumberland, Yorkshire and Cheshire.

In 1900/01 Tom scored 13 tries in 31 games for Oldham, four of which were scored in a Cup-tie against Otley. Oldham challenged strongly for the double but fell in the semi-final of the Challenge Cup to Batley. Tom earned a Lancashire Senior Competition winner's medal though, when, for their last game of the season, Oldham travelled to Cumberland needing to beat Millom to take the title. A 3-0 victory did the trick.

Tom returned to play for Seaton for the next four years, rekindling his career with Cumberland County and acting as an intermediary between Oldham and a gaggle of notable Cumbrian players who all made their way to Watersheddings. In April 1905, Tom returned for a final year with Oldham, playing in the last match of the season, a 23-0 home win over Hull, which secured the First Division Championship for the Roughyeds. A year later, on 4 April 1906, he played his 100th and final game for Oldham at Leigh, having scored 31 tries and 3 goals.

In the next eight years Tom played for Workington, Maryport, Barrow and finally again for Seaton. He became the Grand Old Man of Cumberland rugby and continued to play at county level, despite being well into his thirties. In 1907/08 he was in the Cumberland XIII which lifted the NU County Championship for the first time with

a 7-3 win over Yorkshire at Whitehaven and was also in the teams which beat both the pioneering New Zealanders in 1908 and the first Kangaroos in 1909.

Remarkably, Tom Fletcher was recalled into the Cumberland team for the fixture against Yorkshire at Workington's Lonsdale Park on 11 October 1913. Four years had elapsed since his last appearance and fifteen since his county debut. He lined up opposite the celebrated 'Prince of Centres', Harold Wagstaff, who had been a seven year old when Tom had first played for Cumberland back in 1898. That afternoon thirty-nine- year-old Tom must have felt like a king as he scored one of Cumberland's two tries in an 8-3 victory over the Tykes.

Tom Fletcher was still playing during the First World War, even putting in the odd guest appearances for Oldham, although they were not designated as first-class fixtures. He died on 28 August 1950 at High Harrington.

Jack Flynn

Stand-off, wing, centre

First-class debut
3 September 1904, Swinton v. Wigan (away)
Last game
18 October 1913,
Swinton v. Widnes (away) Lancashire Cup
Cumberland debut
15 October 1904, v. Cheshire at Birkenhead
Cumberland caps
14, 1904-10
England caps
1
Clubs
Swinton, Broughton Rangers

Jack 'Dandy' Flynn was one of the 'person-ality' players of the Edwardian era, apparently having as many detractors as admirers. When he was good he was brilliant, but when he was bad he was awful. Fortunately, he was generally good.

Jack was a native of Whitehaven and played for the local Recs and later Parton. He turned professional with Swinton in 1904 and made his debut on the wing in a 5-2 victory at Wigan. Swinton tended to use him in the three-quarters but he was more suited to stand-off. Jack played two full seasons at Swinton, kicking 21 goals and scoring four tries in 61 appearances, his best match perfor-mance being six goals and a try in a 39-0 home win against Barrow on 30 December 1905.

In 1906 he transferred to Broughton Rangers, who recognised his abilities as a half-back, for in 111 appearances for them, 99 were at stand-off. He scored 19 tries and two goals for Broughton. Within three months Jack had picked up a winner's medal for the Lancashire Cup, scoring a try and dropping a goal in Rangers' 15-6 defeat of Warrington at Central Park, Wigan. In 1907/08, however, he had a most frustrating time as Rangers lost 16-9 in the Lancashire Cup final to Oldham at Rochdale, were runners-up in the Lancashire League and lost twice to Hunslet (in the Challenge Cup semi-final and the Championship semi-final), within a week at the close of the campaign.

He did, however, win his England cap when New Zealand were thrillingly beaten 18-16 at Wigan on 11 January 1908. Three other Cumbrians – Lomas (Salford), Ferguson (Oldham) and Beetham (Broughton Rangers) – were also in the side. A pen picture prior to the game said, 'Flynn can punt effectively with either foot, and is what I should describe as a bustling outside half-back who, if supported effectively, will cause trouble to defenders.'

Jack was a regular for Cumberland between 1904 and 1910, playing at wing, centre and stand-off. In 1907/08 he and Jim Lomas formed a highly effective half-back pairing, guiding Cumberland to the County Championship with victories over Lancashire at Broughton, his home ground, and Yorkshire at Whitehaven, his home town, both by 7-3. He was also a member of the teams which shared the County Championship in 1905/06 and 1909/10.

On 6 February 1909, Jack scored a crucial try in Broughton's 12-10 victory over the first Kangaroos but was back playing for Swinton within two years, making his reappearance in a 5-2 home win over Ebbw Vale on 28 January 1911. He only played another 19 games (three tries) in his second spell at Swinton as his career petered out. Like many of his playing-mates, Jack joined up in the First World War. He was one of twelve Swinton players who were killed in the carnage of 1914-18.

First-class debut
2 May 1960, Workington Town v.
Featherstone Rovers (home)
Last game
29 April 1973,
Oldham v. Dewsbury (away), Play-off
Cumberland debut
25 September 1963, v. Yorkshire at
Wakefield
Cumberland caps
8, 1963-72
Test caps
1
Clubs
Workington Town, Hull KR, Bradford
Northern, Barrow, Oldham

The pen picture in the programme for the 1966 Yorkshire Cup final summed up Frank Foster pretty succinctly. It said he was 'fearless, tireless (and) sets a great example of non-stop aggression.' Thirty-odd years later, Workington Town's greatest administrator, Tom Mitchell, wrote in his memoirs that Frank Foster 'was pound for pound the hardest of forwards.'

That programme writer and Tom Mitchell knew what they were on about. Even today, almost thirty years after Frank played his last match, fans and opponents have no difficulty in recalling Frank Foster and the way he played the game, as one of the most fearsome forwards of the 1960s and early 1970s. Frank belonged to that now almost extinct breed of packmen whom crowds hated and loved simultaneously, the enforcer who could also play masterful rugby football. He was poured from the mould that shaped icons such as Arthur Clues, Artie Beetson, Derek Turner and Malcolm Reilly – mixers and mesmerists, the once-seen-never-forgotten brigade.

Frank played his amateur Rugby League with Grasslot and was such an outstanding loose-forward prospect that he was capped by England at Under 19 level against France at Wigan on 18 April 1959, helping his team to an 18-8 victory. Just over a year later he made a try-scoring debut for Workington Town in a 17-7 home win over Featherstone Rovers.

By 1962 he was a fixture at the back of Town's pack, although leading from the front might be a better way to describe Frank's style. Town were still a formidable team in this period and had qualified for the newly instituted First Division. Their ranks included such luminaries as Brian Edgar, the Martins, Norm Herbert, Syd Lowdon, Ike Southward and the inseperable halves, Sol Roper and Harry Archer. Season 1962/63 saw the introduction of the Western Division Championship and Frank was a key man in Town's drive to the final in which they defeated Widnes 10-0 at Wigan in a replay after a 9-9 draw.

Frank was a very competent goal-kicker, landing 33 for Town in 1962/63 but having his best season with the boot in 1963/64 when he kicked 68. Included amongst them was his best-ever haul of eight in a 43-9 home rout of Hunslet. Whilst place-kicking became a less important part of Frank's armoury as the years wore on – largely because he always played in teams with superb kickers – he always maintained the knack of dropping goals at crucial times.

By 1965 Frank was drawing envious eyes from many of the major clubs. He played his last game for Town on 23 January 1965 sharing the second row with Brian Edgar. The pair scored all Town's points in an 11-7 home win over Leigh, Frank booting four goals and

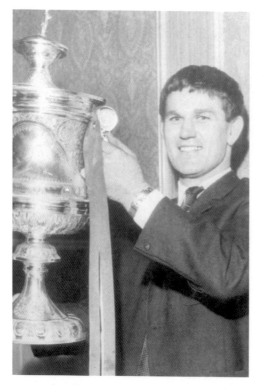

Yorkshire Cup, this time in a nail-biting 8-7 triumph over arch-rivals Hull. Frank actually came off the bench at half-time in this encounter, the only occasion he ever took the field as a substitute. Three weeks later Frank packed down with his club-mates Bill Holliday and Flash Flanagan on his test debut for Great Britain against Australia at London's White City Stadium. The Aussies won a close encounter 17-11 and Frank never got another chance at test rugby. It was Britain's loss.

The close of the season saw Rovers in fine form as they stormed through to their first Championship final since 1925. This time Headingley proved unlucky for Frank and his team as Wakefield Trinity won 17-10 in a splendid game. Within a few months Frank had left for pastures new at Bradford Northern, where he joined forces with, among others, Tony Fisher and Jim Mills. The prospect of facing that trio must have made many sides shudder.

His sojourn at Odsal was, however, to be short. In December 1969 he moved to Barrow with whom he played for almost two years. He finally came to rest at Oldham, making his debut at Whitehaven on 15 January 1972. Oldham used him at blind-side prop and his form and influence elevated him to almost messianic status at Watersheddings. When he arrived, Oldham were in the doldrums having only 13 points from 21 games. By the season's end, they had lost only one more game out of thirteen and qualified for the play-offs. Frank was a miracle-worker.

The Oldham historian, Michael Turner summed up Frank Foster's contribution at Watersheddings most aptly, 'Frank was that strange enigma of being as tricky and skilful as any halfback, while remaining the toughest and most uncompromising of prop forwards...In over 35 years of watching the club, I would say that no player has ever made the same immediate and positive impression on the club as did Frank Foster...He had the knack of committing several defenders to the tackle and then releasing the ball from almost impossible situations. Also possessing a tremendous field kicking game, he was an awesome all-round talent who led from the front with never a backward step.'

Brian grabbing the only try. A week later a massive fee of £6,500 took Frank to Hull Kingston Rovers where he joined another Cumbrian star, Bill Holliday, who had left Whitehaven for an even larger fee a couple of weeks earlier. Frank made his debut for Rovers on 6 February 1965 in a first round Challenge Cup-tie against lowly Batley, who caused one of the biggest upsets in the history of the competition by winning 7-5.

Fortunately things improved markedly for Frank and his new team. Rovers quickly saw leadership qualities in him and he was appointed captain in 1965/66. The following season his men won the Mackeson Competition as the most prolific scoring team in the league and Frank was chosen as Player of the Year. More importantly, he led Rovers to second place in the Championship and skippered them to success in the Yorkshire Cup final with a convincing 25-12 win over Featherstone at Leeds.

The next season (1967/68) saw Frank Foster possibly at his best. On 14 October at Headingley he again led Rovers to success in the

Tom Gainford

Loose-forward, second-rower

First-class debut
1 January 1968, Whitehaven v. Barrow (home)
Last game
24 August 1980,
Barrow v. Warrington (home) Lancashire Cup
Cumberland debut
24 September 1969,
v. Lancashire at Workington
Cumberland caps
6, 1969-78
Clubs
Whitehaven, Barrow

Whitehaven were destined to make a colossal profit when they signed Kells amateur Tom Gainford for £125 in 1967. Tom went on to become one of the most consistent, hard-working and popular loose-forwards or second-rowers ever seen at the Recreation Ground. His forte was a remarkably effective tackling game, never sparing his 6ft 1in, thirteen stone frame.

He made his first-team debut at loose-forward on New Year's Day 1968 in a 15-5 home defeat by Barrow. For over a decade he was a mainstay of the Whitehaven pack, making 284 appearances (21 tries) for the club, almost equally divided between second-row and number thirteen.

Whitehaven were largely unsuccessful in Tom's time but there were some high points. One was the victory over Wigan in the Championship play-offs in 1970, when, after a startling 20-20 draw at Central Park, 'Haven won the replay 9-4. Tom's defensive display at Wigan was awesome. Leeds knocked 'Haven out in the quarter-final. In 1971 Tom played against the Kiwis, who defeated Whitehaven 21-8, and in 1973 the team reached the Lancashire Cup semi-final but lost at home to St Helens. In 1972/73 Whitehaven had performed beyond expectations by finishing 15th of the 30 league clubs to qualify for the newly-formed First Division but were relegated after only one season.

In 1974 Tom played his last really big game for the club, when Whitehaven fought their way into the semi-final of the John Player Trophy only to lose 18-6 at home to Bradford

Northern, the eventual trophy winners.

In 1975/76 Tom played in all 29 of the club's fixtures, a rare feat. His last game for Whitehaven was on 17 December 1978 against Dewsbury at the Rec. He had been transfer-listed at a huge £12,500, recognition that he was perhaps the best uncapped back-row forward in the game. Both Barrow and Leigh offered £9,000, and Tom chose to join Barrow, who were spending heavily to retain their First Division status. A measure of Tom's standing was reflected in the fact that Barrow had just signed test star Bob Irving from Salford for £9,000.

Tom settled in well at loose-forward but Barrow just failed to avoid relegation. The 1979/80 season, however, saw them promoted again and there was a near miss as Barrow lost 6-4 to Workington in the Lancashire Cup semi-final. Tom played 41 games for Barrow (two tries) but was injured in the first game of the 1980/81 season and never played again.

Tom's county career was truncated by injuries after he had made his debut against Lancashire in 1969. He did not play for Cumbria again until 1975 – it had been Cumberland when he started – and he did not finish on a winning side until his last game, a 16-15 success against Lancashire at Whitehaven in 1978.

Billy Garratt
Stand-off, centre

First-class debut
19 August 1950, Whitehaven v. Oldham (home)
Last game
6 December 1958,
Whitehaven v. Keighley (away)
Cumberland debut
1 October 1951,
v. Yorkshire at Craven Park, Hull
Cumberland caps
6, 1951-58
Club
Whitehaven

Many life-long followers of Whitehaven will swear blind that Billy Garratt was the best stand-off the club has ever had – and they have had some good ones. Why he never gained full international honours remains a mystery to them.

Billy played amateur Rugby League for Kells and was capped by England (Under 21) against France at Avignon on 23 April 1950. The game was lost 17-0 but less than a year later he was on the winning side in a professional Under 21 international at Wigan on 10 March 1951, when England beat France 23-7.

By then Billy was Whitehaven's stand-off, striking up a productive partnership with scrum-half Tommy Keen, which would only end when Tommy suffered a severe neck injury in 1956. As a stand-off Billy had most of the necessary qualities. He was elusive and creative, a good tactician who was adept at the cross-kick and an astute touch-finder. His side-on tackling was a feature of his play and many of the best stand-offs of his time came off second best in their clashes with him. Possibly the major factor in his failure to gain the highest representative honours was a lack of blistering pace.

Billy stood about 5ft 9in tall and eventually weighed over 13st, allowing him to perform well at centre, in which position he played 63 of his 234 games for Whitehaven. He claimed 42 tries in his time at the Recreation Ground.

His versatility was well illustrated in his appearances for Cumberland. In his debut, a 25-3 defeat by Yorkshire at Craven Park, Hull in 1951, he played scrum-half to Russ Pepperell. His next match against Lancashire, on the Recreation Ground, on 12 May 1952 saw him at centre. Three games followed at stand-off and in his sixth and final game for the county, a 29-7 rout of Yorkshire at Whitehaven on 15 September 1958, he successfully filled the loose-forward berth. In the 15-14 win over Yorkshire at Whitehaven on 19 September 1956, Billy was one of no fewer than eight Whitehaven players in the Cumberland XIII.

Billy was captain of the outstanding 1956/57 Whitehaven side which beat the Australians – he had also played against the 1952 Kangaroos – and reached the Challenge Cup semi-finals. His partnership with the veteran Welsh scrum-half Billy Banks played a large part in 'Haven's success.

In his last season at Whitehaven Billy was moved from stand-off to loose-forward, playing there for the first time on 16 August 1958 in a 51-12 home victory over York. For a short time he formed a very useful back row with any two from John Tembey, Geoff Robinson and Dick Huddart. Unfortunately, a back injury brought his season to a premature close and then a career move to Rhodesia ended this popular player's association with Whitehaven.

Eppie Gibson
Centre

First-class debut
23 August 1947,
Workington Town v. Dewsbury (home)
Last game
3 April 1961,
Whitehaven v. Workington Town (away)
Cumberland debut
22 October 1947, v. Yorkshire at Leeds
Cumberland caps
17, 1947-59
England caps
4
Clubs
Workington Town, Whitehaven

Of all the centres produced by Cumberland in the post-war period none has been more widely admired than Edward 'Eppie' Gibson. Eppie was not the biggest of centres at around 5ft 10in and 12st 7lbs, but he was one of the classiest. Alan Cave wrote of him, 'Here was a centre in the old classic mould, a man who could make openings out of nothing, a man who by dint of side-step and swerve could wriggle out of trouble, and make it for the other side.'

Although outstanding as an attacker, Eppie was almost as good a defender. Moreover, he was a clean, sporting player who developed into an admirable captain and coach.

Eppie was born in Northumberland in 1927 but moved to Cumberland in the first weeks of his infancy. Brought up in Ellenborough and educated at Cockermouth Grammar School, he played some amateur Rugby League for Brookland Rovers but earned a big reputation playing Rugby Union for Loughborough College, England Universities and Cumberland.

Workington Town signed him in July 1947 and he was straightaway put into the fiirst team at stand-off, where he made such an impression that within two months he had played for Cumberland and England, as meteoric a rise as the game has ever seen.

His county debut, alongside Town's scrum-half Albert Pepperell, was a triumph. Cumberland overcame Yorkshire 15-7 at Leeds, Eppie played a stormer, scoring a crucial try, and outplayed the Yorkshire captain Ron Rylance, who unfortunately was injured, having already been selected for England's game against France at Fartown three days later. The selectors had seen enough in the county game and drafted Eppie into the England team to partner Tommy Bradshaw. He finished on the winning side, 20-15, and made a try for second-rower Len Aston. However, it would be another four years before the nineteen year old would gain another international cap.

Eppie's county career stretched over a dozen years and brought him seventeen caps. In his second game on 13 October 1948, he had the rare pleasure of being in a team that beat the Australians 5-4 at Whitehaven. A rumpus then blew up about his eligibility for the county on account of his Northumberland birth, causing him to miss several games until it was decided that he was, after all, entitled to represent Cumberland. The problem cost him a County Championship winner's medal for 1948/49. It was not until the 1959/60 season that Cumberland again won the title.

continued unabated, as Gus Risman built the side into one that challenged for honours. Eppie moved into Town's centres, where from 1949 he forged a formidable partnership with the Australian Tony Paskins which often caused havoc for other teams. The wings were test man Johnny Lawrenson and the flying Scot, George 'Happy' Wilson, who played outside Eppie.

Eppie's most productive season was arguably 1950/51. He and George Wilson both racked up 40 tries. Eppie scored four in a 56-2 win against York at Borough Park and hat-tricks in away games at Belle Vue Rangers, Liverpool Stanley and Barrow. Forty tries by a centre in any era is a phenomenal achievement. The two that really counted though were scored on 12 May 1951, at Maine Road, where Town defeated Warrington 26-11 to lift the Championship in the first major final contested by Workington. He made two other tries and played one of the games of his life.

The following season he only scored seven tries but creation was now the name of his game, as the regular three-quarter line amassed 108 tries between them. Again the campaign ended in glory, as Eppie figured in Town's wonderful Wembley victory over Featherstone Rovers in the Challenge Cup final. Town continued to test the best and in 1955 they were back at Wembley against Willie Horne's Barrow. Town were well beaten 21-12 but Eppie scored the last and best try of the game. His play was described by one critic as 'brilliant on attack'.

After 335 games for Town, in which he totalled 145 tries and 19 goals, Eppie transferred to Whitehaven, for whom he made his debut on 27 August 1957, in an 15-8 loss at Rochdale Hornets in a Lancashire Cup-tie. He continued to deliver the goods at The Rec for the next four years, becoming player-coach. During his time in charge, Whitehaven rose to their loftiest eminence, when they finished sixth in the league in 1959/60. He played 88 games for Whitehaven, scoring 20 tries and 15 goals. He scored another try for a combined Whitehaven-Workington XIII against the 1959 Kangaroos. Appropriately enough, if not happily, his last game was at Workington Town, who beat Whitehaven 36-2.

Poetically, that was Eppie's last season as a county player and he was skipper of the team that beat Lancashire at Workington and Yorkshire at Hull – a fitting finale for one of Cumberland's great men.

At international level Eppie was probably undervalued. He did add three further England caps to his tally – against Other Nationalties at Wigan in 1951, when England lost heavily, and in victorious games against Wales at St Helens in 1951 and against Other Nationalities at Wigan in 1953. He scored tries in both the latter fixtures. In 1954 he was regarded as a good bet for a Lions tour and figured in the second tour trial for the Whites against the Reds at Swinton on 10 March. The selectors decided to pick all four centres who had appeared in the first trial at Headingley three weeks earlier! Eppie never did win a test cap. He must certainly have been among the very finest of centres to have suffered that fate.

Nonetheless his success at Workington

Les Gorley
Second-rower

First-class debut
17 March 1971,
Workington Town v. Oldham (away)
Last game
11 May 1986, Whitehaven v. Bramley (away)
Cumberland debut
17 January 1973, v. Yorkshire at Leeds
Cumberland caps
16, 1973-81
England caps
2
Test caps
5
Clubs
Workington Town, Widnes, Whitehaven

Cumberland has produced few better all-round forwards than Les Gorley, who was born in 1950 and hailed from Great Broughton. He had all the power and determination associated with the great Cumbrian packmen. Moreover, he had the physique to impose himself on any opposition, standing 6ft 2in and weighing around 14st at the beginning of his career and 16st at the end. For such a big man he was very mobile and piled up over 80 tries in his career.

Les was not just a powerhouse second-rower, though. He was a gifted ball-handler, full of guile and a master at slipping the one-handed pass.

His career began at Workington Town in 1971 and he gave the club eight years' sterling service, roaring over for 50 tries, including two hat-tricks, in 224 games. He also kicked a couple of goals against Oldham in his debut year but never kicked another. Les played in three consecutive Lancashire Cup finals for Town (1976, 1977 and 1978), helping them to win the trophy for the only time in 1977.

In 1979 he moved to Widnes for £18,000, making his debut in a Lancashire Cup-tie victory at St Helens on 19 August. Widnes were the Cup Kings of the period and Les enjoyed enormous success in his five years at Naughton Park. Ironically, the first medal he won as a Chemic was for Widnes's 11-0 triumph over Workington in the 1979 Lancashire Cup final. He also won a runners-up medal for the Players Trophy and crowned his first season at Widnes by scoring a try in the 19-5 Premiership final victory over Bradford Northern at Swinton.

In 1981 Les won at Wembley, Hull KR being defeated 18-9 in the Challenge Cup final. In 1982 he was back but Widnes drew with Hull and lost the replay at Elland Road. A third Challenge Cup final in 1984 ended more happily as Wigan were beaten 19-6 in Les's 162nd and last game for the club. He had also picked up two more Premiership winners' medals in 1981/82 and 1982/83, and runners-up medals for the Lancashire Cup finals of 1981 and 1983 and for the Players Trophy in 1983/84.

Les's club career concluded in Cumberland with a couple of seasons at Whitehaven, where he made 47 appearances (eight tries), finally making the transition to prop after fourteen years in the second-row.

At international level Les played twice for England, against Wales at Headingley in 1977 and at Cardiff in 1981. His test career yielded five caps beginning with a 14-14 draw against New Zealand at Wigan in 1980. However, it ended traumatically with a dismissal against France at Marseilles in 1981 and that cataclysmic 40-4 defeat by the Australian Invincibles at Boothferry Park, Hull, in the first Ashes test of 1982.

Peter Gorley
Second-row, loose-forward, prop

First-class debut
2 November 1975, Workington Town v.
Blackpool Borough (away)
Last game
12 October 1986,
Whitehaven v. Doncaster (away)
Cumbria debut
5 October 1977, v. Yorkshire at York
Cumbria caps
8, 1977-82
England caps
3
Test caps
3
Clubs
Workington Town, St Helens, Whitehaven

It was no fun going to Cumberland and being grabbed by the Gorleys, to coin a phrase. Peter Gorley was Les's younger brother by a year. Like Les, he had played amateur Rugby League for Broughton Red Rose and had turned professional with Workington Town. He was only a smidgeon smaller than Les and developed into one of the most outstanding second-rowers of his era. He was a real dynamo, a damaging forward in both attack and defence. Peter, however, played in a wider variety of pack positions, playing some of his early career at loose-forward, his later career at prop and once even turned out at hooker for Town.

He made his debut for Workington in 1975 and made 124 appearances for the club over four years, scoring thirteen tries. He played alongside his brother in the three Lancashire Cup finals of 1976, 1977 and 1978 before moving to St Helens for a fee of £22,000. He made a try-scoring debut for Saints on 9 October 1979 in a 45-17 home victory over Rochdale Hornets in a Floodlit Trophy tie.

Although St Helens were one of the game's top clubs, surprisingly Peter did not win many trophies in his time at Knowsley Road. He certainly did his share, scoring 46 tries in 234 matches but luck seemed to be against Saints in this period. In 1982 Peter appeared in his fourth Lancashire Cup final but Warrington dispatched Saints 16-0 at Wigan.

In 1984 Saints clicked, galvanised by the arrival of Mal Meninga. Peter had moved to blind-side prop and many critics believe he had never played more devastatingly than in the 1984/85 season.

Saints began by lifting the Lancashire Cup, recording a 26-18 victory over Wigan in the final, despite the game being played at Central Park, Wigan's home ground. At the season's end Peter won his biggest domestic honour as Saints ripped Hull KR apart 36-16 at Elland Road, Leeds, in the 1985 Premiership final.

He played his last game as a Saint on 2 February 1986 in a 44-14 home win against Featherstone Rovers. A couple of months later he made his debut for Whitehaven in a 12-10 success at Workington Town but only played three games before retiring.

In representative rugby in 1981 Peter played alongside Les for Cumbria, England and Great Britain. The brothers were in Cumbria's second-row when the County Championship was won. They played together in England's 20-15 win over Wales at Cardiff on 8 November 1981, with Peter claiming a try, and six weeks later shared the second-row duties in a 37-0 thrashing of France at The Boulevard, Hull. All Peter's six international and test caps were won as a second-rower in 1980 and 1981, while his career for Cumbria included an appearance against Lancashire at loose-forward.

Vince Gribbin
Winger, centre

First-class debut
10 October 1982,
Whitehaven v. Hunslet (away)
Last game
21 April 1996, Whitehaven v. Featherstone
Rovers (home)
Cumbria debut
5 November 1991,
v. Papua-New Guinea at Workington
Cumbria caps
1, 1991
Test caps
1
Clubs
Whitehaven, Salford (loan)

Records were meant to be broken. At least that seems to have been the philosophy of Vince Gribbin, who rewrote many at Whitehaven.

Vince signed for Whitehaven on 23 July 1982, having played as an amateur with Hensingham. His career started in the grand manner with eighteen points (two tries, five goals) on his debut at Hunslet. In his first season, 26 games all on the wing, brought him eleven tries and fifty goals for 'Haven, who won promotion. He was clearly something else. He had exceptional pace and an insatiable urge to score tries, often of the spectacular variety. His second season was less prolific – eight tries and 48 goals – but in 1984/85, having moved to centre, he racked up 25 tries and 23 goals. Among the tries were a club record six in a Regal Trophy tie against Doncaster, who were hammered 64-0. The six were also a competition record. Vince had run in three at Bridgend the previous week.

In October 1985 Vince went to Salford on loan, played four games and scored three tries. He then returned to Whitehaven and promptly gave up the game after playing in a 28-0 home win over Mansfield on 8 December 1985. He had played 81 games for the club bagging 45 tries and 121 goals.

Vince had not yet turned twenty-one and he had the Rugby League world at his feet. He had been capped twice by Great Britain against France at Under 21 level, scoring the only try of the game in an 8-2 victory at Albi

on 16 December 1984, when he partnered Garry Schofield in the centre. A few months later, on 1 March 1985, he had scorched 45 yards for a super try at Headingley on his full test debut in a 50-4 rout of France. No Whitehaven player has since won a test cap.

After a break of four years, Vince made his reappearance for Whitehaven on 3 September 1989 as a substitute against Huddersfield. He was soon back in the scoring groove. In 1991/92 he shattered Bill Smith's club record of 29 tries set back in 1956/57. With three games to go, he needed to score a seemingly impossible nine tries to beat the record. Two at Trafford Borough, three at Keighley and five in an 80-6 home massacre of Nottingham City did the trick and established a new record of 31. Mark Pechey broke Vince's record with 34 in 1994/95.

In 1992/93 Vince scored 22 tries in 22 games, including five against Blackpool and four against Highfield, both games being 72-0 victories. By the time he finished at Whitehaven in 1996 he had scored 801 points (142 tries, 122 goals) in 215 games for the club. But for his early career break, he may have set unbreakable records.

First-class debut
25 August 1945, Workington Town v.
Broughton Rangers (home)
Last game
17 December 1955, Workington Town v.
Bradford Northern (home)
Cumberland debut
26 September 1946, v. Yorkshire at Workington
Cumberland caps
16, 1946-55
England caps
1
Club
Workington Town

Workington Town's first signing took place on 7 July 1945 and the signing-on fee was £25. For that Town got ten years' service and 366 first-team appearances from Jimmy Hayton from Broughton Moor. Bargains do not come much cheaper than that.

Jimmy had already played at Borough Park as a second-rower for a Cumberland XIII against an England XIII on 12 May 1945 in a kind of taster before professional Rugby League was launched in Workington. His performance clearly impressed the Town directorate and when Town played their first league game against Broughton Rangers on 25 August 1945, Jimmy was at open-side prop in a 27-5 victory.

In his first few years in the game he alternated between second-row and prop but by 1948/49 had settled at blind-side prop, moving permanently to open-side in November 1950. At 5ft 9in and 15st 4lbs, Jimmy was ideally suited to his position. He was an excellent scrummager, robust, hard in the tackle and hard to tackle. Few opposing forwards would take liberties with him.

Jimmy took part in most of Workington's big games in their first decade of existence. He played in their first game against a touring team, when Town went down 7-12 to the 1947 Kiwis and was in the team that beat the 1948 Kangaroos 10-7. There were disappointments in the Lancashire Cup, Jimmy playing in four losing semi-finals in 1947, 1949, 1952 and 1954.

They were more than compensated for, however, by the momentous events of 1951 and 1952. In 1951 Jimmy was hard at work in the front-row boiler house as Town swept Warrington away 26-11 in a gloriously entertaining Championship final at Maine Road, Manchester. The following year in another excellent game he earned a Challenge Cup winner's medal when Town defeated Featherstone Rovers 18-10. Wembley beckoned again in 1955 but this time Jimmy and his colleagues had to accept runners-up medals as Barrow beat Town 21-12.

Eight months after the 1955 Challenge Cup final Jimmy had retired, his 366 appearances for the club being a record. He had scored 29 tries.

Jimmy was certainly one of the top props of the immediate post-war era but was only capped once by England. On 19 September 1949, he turned out in the first international played by the Other Nationalities, who beat England 13-7 at Borough Park. His pack-mate Billy Ivison was in the England team while other Town players Tony Paskins and Johnny Mudge were in the opposition. In May 1951 Jimmy propped in a United Kingdom XIII's 13-10 victory over a French XIII in Paris.

At county level Jimmy was a stalwart for nine years, gaining a County Championship winner's medal in 1948/49, and participating in Cumberland's great 5-4 victory over the Australians at Whitehaven on 13 October 1948.

John Henderson
Prop, second-row forward

First-class debut
2 April 1951, Workington Town v. Liverpool
Stanley (home)
Last game
17 October 1959, York v. Keighley (away)
Cumberland debut
12 May 1952, v. Lancashire at Whitehaven
Cumberland caps
8, 1952-57
England caps
1
Clubs
Workington Town, Halifax, York

John Henderson was not a ball-playing, try-scoring, spectacular running forward, not an eye-catcher, but he was a hell of a prop or second-rower. He was the type all good packs need – a worker, who would tackle, take the ball up and graft for the full 80 minutes. Strong, hard, rugged, with legs like tree trunks, John was a prime exponent of solid Cumbrian forward play.

Born in Maryport in 1929, he joined Workington Town in 1950 but had to bide his time before breaking into arguably the best club side Cumberland ever produced. Town won the Championship in 1950/51 and John figured in just his debut game, 29-11 home win over Liverpool Stanley, when he formed the front row with old stagers Vince McKeating and Jimmy Hayton. His second game was against the New Zealanders on 24 September 1951 at open-side prop, opposite the Kiwi legend Cliff Johnson. By the season's close he was forcing himself into the Town team, which made history by winning the Challenge Cup. John earned a winner's medal by appearing in the third round 14-0 victory over Warrington, when 19,720 crammed into Borough Park.

He won his first Cumberland cap as a second-rower in an 11-19 defeat by Lancashire at Whitehaven in 1952 and a year later was capped by England at blind-side prop in a 24-5 triumph over Wales at St Helens. His forceful style projected him into the 1954 Lions tour squad, after a good show in the tour trial at Swinton. John played in eleven tour games for Great Britain, including the

notorious affair against New South Wales, when the referee abandoned the game because of brawling.

After playing 107 games for Town, he transferred to Halifax for £2,000 in January 1955, playing another 90 games for them. Included was the Yorkshire Cup final of 1955 against Hull, when he scored the first try and was sent off! The game ended in a 10-10 draw. John missed the replay which Halifax won 7-0. He did, however, gain a Yorkshire League winner's medal later that season and played in Halifax's defeats in both the Challenge Cup final and the Championship final.

In 1956 John played in a famous 6-3 Halifax victory over the Australians – the last time Halifax beat the Aussies – and also toured France with the club, when they defeated Albi and Carcassonne in European Championship games. His last season at Thrum Hall, 1957/58, brought him a second Yorkshire League winner's medal.

The 5ft 10.5in and 15st forward made a final move to York, at a fee of £2,700, making his debut on 1 February 1958 in a stunning 31-7 victory at Warrington. He played exactly 50 games for the Minstermen.

Martin Hodgson

Second-row forward

First-class debut
16 April 1927, Swinton v. St Helens (away)
Last game
9 May 1942,
Bradford Northern v. Halifax (home), Cup
Cumberland debut
24 September 1927,
v. Lancashire at Whitehaven
Cumberland caps
29, 1927-38
England caps
9
Test caps
16
Club
Swinton

Martin Hodgson was loved, feared and respected throughout the northern Rugby League playing counties in the inter-war years. He was a forward fit to rank with any the game has produced. Yet his fame, particularly in the 1930s, was probably as pronounced in Australia as it was in Cumberland, Lancashire and Yorkshire. In five consecutive Ashes series the Australians had developed an unholy dread of Hodgson. It seemed they were incapable of defeating Britain in a test series as long as Martin was in the British jersey. The facts confirm the Aussies' apprehension, for in a dozen Ashes tests Martin was on the losing side only twice.

On his two Lions tours Down Under in 1932 and 1936 the Australian crowds were stupefied by Martin's performances. The Australian press, drawing parallels from the notorious Bodyline cricket test series of 1932/33, demonised Martin in 1936 into a sort of Harold Larwood figure. He became the man who terrorised Australia – the English bogey-man. Martin Hodgson was a hard player, certainly, but by no means vicious. Back home English Rugby League followers thought that the Australian scribes would have had more mileage out of Martin's fellow second-rower, Jack Arkwright of Warrington, who undoubtedly had a reputation for skullduggery.

Whatever the views of the Australians by 1936, Martin Hodgson's Rugby League career had begun a long time previously back home

in West Cumberland. Born in Egremont in 1909, Martin had begun his rugby career as a union player with the local club. He had already won county honours when Swinton signed him on 8 January 1927, a couple of months before his eighteenth birthday. He was joining arguably the sport's pre-eminent club at this period. His first-team debut resulted in a 27-0 defeat at St Helens. Despite this inauspicious start, within little more than a year he had been capped by Cumberland and England and had won all the major domestic honours open to him. The world of Rugby League was at his feet.

During his first full season with Swinton, Martin played in 43 of the club's 48 fixtures, as they swept all before them to become the third and last team to win all four of the game's traditional cups, emulating the wonderful exploits of Hunslet in 1907/08 and Huddersfield in 1914/15. Apart from winning the Lancashire League Championship, Swinton defeated Wigan 5-2 in the Lancashire Cup final, Warrington 5-3 in the Challenge Cup final and Featherstone Rovers 11-0 in the Championship final, with Martin in the second-row on each occasion.

There would be further winners' medals for Martin with Swinton in the Lancashire League in 1928/29, 1930/31 and 1939/40, while he would win Lancashire Cup medals for the finals of 1931 (runners-up) and 1940 (winners), by which time he was the Swinton captain.

Apart from being a truly awesome forward – at 6ft 1in and 14st he was a very big man for the times – and one of the best cover-tacklers of his era, Martin Hodgson was a prodigious goal-kicker. Some of his best goal-kicking performances were achieved in major matches. For example, it was Martin's four goals which materially enabled Swinton to beat Leeds 14-7 at Wigan in the Championship final of 1931, a feat he repeated on the same ground in the Championship final of 1935 when Warrington were defeated 14-3. He was less fortunate in 1932, however, again at Wigan, in the Challenge Cup final, when both he and the Leeds captain, Joe Thompson, booted four penalty goals, as Leeds scored the only try to take the Cup 11-8.

Martin's goal-kicking was a massive boost for any team in which he appeared and for many years the record books credited him with the longest goal ever kicked – in a Lancashire Cup-tie at Rochdale Hornets on 13 April 1940. The distance from launch to landing was estimated at over 77 yards. Modern researchers have, however, recently decided that the distance from kick to cross-bar was in fact 58 yards. Whatever the real distance, Martin's place amongst the great goal-kickers of history is assured. For Swinton alone he landed 862 goals in 473 appearances and in his first-class career (576 games) his total was 995 goals. That makes him the second most prolific Cumbrian goal-kicker of all-time behind Whitehaven's John McKeown, who amassed 1,092.

At representative level Martin Hodgson was almost indispensable for Cumberland, England and the test XIII for practically the whole of his career. His debut for Cumberland in a 27-2 rout of Lancashire at Whitehaven in 1927 marked the beginning of an unbroken run of 29 appearances for the county which only ended when the Second World War brought the County Championship to a halt. Martin took over the Cumberland captaincy from Jim Brough in 1936 and was a member of four Cumberland County Championship-winning sides.

Martin won nine England caps in home internationals against Wales and France between 1928 and 1937, and was captain twice. His test record was phenomenal for he appeared in successful Ashes-winning squads in 1929/30, 1932, 1933, 1936 and 1937 – a feat unparalleled by any other British forward. His durability and value to the national team was never more clearly witnessed than on the Lions tours of 1932 and 1936. On the 1932 trip he played in all six tests and, together with Albert Fildes (St Helens), played 19 tour matches – more than any other forward. In 1936 he again topped the appearances with 18 and, moreover, led the tour scorers with 139 points (3 tries, 65 goals).

On Christmas Day 1940, Martin played his last game for Swinton in a 16-5 victory at Oldham but continued to play as a guest for Bradford Northern, Huddersfield and Hunslet until 1942, when he finally retired, aged thirty-three. He had done everything and won everything – repeatedly. If ever a Cumbrian Rugby League Hall of Fame is instituted, Martin Hodgson would certainly be a prime candidate.

Billy Holding

Full-back

First-class debut
21 January 1928, Warrington v. York (home)
Last game
7 September 1946, Workington Town v.
Oldham (home), Lancashire Cup
Cumberland debut
9 December 1929, v. Australians at
Workington
Cumberland caps
14, 1929-38
Clubs
Warrington, Rochdale Hornets, Salford
(wartime guest), Workington Town

Billy Holding, from Maryport, was one of the best goal-kickers Cumberland ever produced. He made his name with Warrington, for whom he landed 834 goals in 327 appearances between 1928 and 1939.

During that time he shattered most of the club records. In 1929/30 he set up a new record with 84 goals; the following season he extended the record to 101 and broke it again in 1932/33 with 125 goals and scored a third century (116) in 1933/34.

Billy enjoyed plenty of success with Warrington. He played in winning Lancashire Cup finals in 1929 and 1932 and gained a winner's medal for the Lancashire League Championship in 1937/38. He won a third Lancashire Cup-winner's medal in 1937 but missed the final victory over Barrow through injury. Injuries also dogged him for other major finals. For example, he played in the Championship finals of 1935 and 1937 only to be crocked in both and to end up with loser's medals.

In 1933 Billy took Warrington to Wembley almost single-footedly. At Wigan in the third round he kicked a last minute touch-line conversion to win the tie 9-7 and then booted four match-winning goals as St Helens were

beaten 11-5 in the semi-final at Swinton. The final against Huddersfield was played before the Prince of Wales, the first royal of the royal family to attend a final. Billy was the sole Cumbrian to figure on this historic occasion. Prior to the game, posters had been put up in London urging people to 'come to Wembley to see Holding, the wonder goal-kicker'. The game was a classic but Warrington lost 17-21. Billy converted all three Wire tries and kicked a penalty.

His biggest disappointment, however, was to occur in 1936 when Warrington again reached Wembley. Billy broke his leg in a first round triumph at Barrow and missed all the remaining cup-ties.

The nearest Billy got to an international cap was in 1933/34 when he was reserve for England. He appeared in tour trials in 1932 and 1936.

At county level, however, Billy Holding turned out to be one of the best. His debut against the Australians at Workington brought a famous 8-5 victory, in which Billy kicked the first of 45 goals for Cumberland. When Billy landed seven goals against Yorkshire at York in 1931, he created a record which stood until 1960.

In 1939/40 he moved to Rochdale Hornets, guested briefly for Salford and retired in 1941. Four years later he re-emerged to play for the newly-founded Workington Town.

Billy Holding scored 975 goals and 1971 points in 393 first-class games. The only Cumbrians to have amassed more goals are Martin Hodgson and John McKeown.

Bill Holliday
Forward

First-class debut
15 August 1959,
Whitehaven v. Huddersfield (home)
Last game
21 April 1974,
Rochdale Hornets v. Widnes (home)
Cumberland debut
9 October 1961,
v. New Zealanders at Whitehaven
Cumberland caps
10, 1961-68
Test caps
10
Clubs
Whitehaven, Hull KR, Swinton, Rochdale
Hornets

Imagine a Rugby League forward who could handle and pass the ball sublimely, lead by example, defend ferociously, shake off injuries which would stop many men in their tracks, kick goals off the half-way line and put the fear of God into opposing packs. Such creatures did exist in Rugby League, although admittedly they were few and far between. When they were discovered they were worth their weight in gold. Bill Holliday was such a player.

Born in Whitehaven in 1939, Bill played his junior rugby with Wath Brow Hornets and was capped as an amateur by England against France at Villeneuve on 1 May 1959. It was the prelude to a wonderful career as a professional which began three months later with Whitehaven, when he made a try-scoring debut in a 17-5 victory over Huddersfield at the Recreation Ground. He established himself in the first team from the off, alternating between second-row and loose-forward.

In his first season Bill played 30 games. One of his earliest matches was for a combined Whitehaven-Workington Town XIII which lost only 8-13 to the Kangaroos, whilst on 19 March 1960 he was in the 'Haven team which went down 10-21 to Wakefield Trinity at the Rec in the third round of the Challenge Cup before 18,650 spectators – the biggest crowd ever to see a game at Whitehaven.

Bill was a fine goal-kicker but, with John McKeown in the team, he got little practice until 1961/62. Thereafter he became the club's main kicker and on 31 March 1962 he set a new points scoring record when he kicked eleven goals and scored a try (25 points) in a 61-0 rout of Hunslet. Bill seemed almost indestructible, hardly ever missing a game. In 1962/63 he played in all 37 of Whitehaven's fixtures, a rare achievement.

His career at Whitehaven spanned almost six seasons, during which he made 188 appearances and amassed 553 points (21 tries, 245 goals). By December 1963 he had played for Cumberland against both the 1961 Kiwis and the 1963 Kangaroos and was club captain. A year later, on 6 December 1964, he won his first test cap against France at Perpignan. By then he was one of the hottest properties in the game and Whitehaven, in one of their many financial crises, let him go to Hull KR for a massive fee approaching £8,000. His last game for 'Haven had seen them draw 3-3 with Bradford Northern at the Rec on 9 January 1965.

Hull KR were developing into one of the game's major powers and Bill was now firmly in the limelight, particularly as he was one

Park had seen him become a regular test player. He had been vice-captain of the Great Britain team that won the 1965 home series against New Zealand and it had been a considerable shock when he was left out of the 1966 Lions tour squad.

In 1967 Rovers had decided that Bill was better suited to open-side prop than to second-row. The Cumberland selectors agreed and Bill landed four crucial goals in the county's superb 17-15 win over the Australians at Workington. Moreover, the Great Britain selectors entrusted him with the captaincy for the entire 1967 Ashes series, which began with a 16-11 triumph at Headingley. The series was lost, however, with defeats at London's White City Stadium and Swinton.

Bill had become only the fourth Cumbrian to skipper Great Britain, his predecessors being Jim Lomas, Jim Brough and Brian Edgar. No Cumbrian has subsequently won this honour and Bill Holliday is the only Whitehaven native to have captained the test XIII.

A £6,000 transfer took Bill to Swinton in September 1968. Swinton were still among the leading clubs at that period and in 1969 Bill was in their second-row when they defeated Leigh 11-2 at Wigan in the Lancashire Cup final. He remained a Swinton player for four years, his last game for them being a second Lancashire Cup final on 21 October 1972. Unfortunately, Salford beat Swinton 25-11 at Warrington.

Bill then made a final move to Rochdale Hornets. Ironically, his debut saw him land three goals in a 9-7 victory at Whitehaven on 26 November 1972. Hornets had assembled a useful team and in Bill's last season, 1973/74, it carried a real sting. Bill kicked 110 goals – his first century – and inspired his men to the Players Trophy final. Although they went down 16-27 to Warrington at Wigan on 9 February 1974, Hornets' very presence in the final had startled the Rugby League world.

Bill Holliday's first-class career came to an end a couple of months later at Rochdale's Athletic Grounds in a Club Championship play-off against Widnes when he landed his 647th goal. It was his 508th senior match and his grand total of 1,438 points was eloquent testimony to a magificent career.

third of a truly formidable back-row with fellow Cumbrian Frank Foster and Harry Poole, who was to captain the 1966 Lions in Australasia. Bill earned Yorkshire Cup winners' medals with Rovers in 1966 and 1967, while in 1968 he was a major influence in Rovers' surge to the Championship final, only for injury to prevent him playing against Wakefield Trinity at Headingley.

That 1967/68 season saw Bill possibly at the height of his powers. He had taken over from Cyril Kellett as Hull KR's goal-kicker, had led Rovers to a 27-15 win over the Kangaroos and had won a number of games through his mastery of the drop-goal, 19 of his 79 goals being dropped. His time at Craven

Les Holliday
Loose-forward

First-class debut
14 December 1982,
Swinton v. Doncaster (home)
Last game
27 July 1997,
Swinton v. Rochdale Hornets (away)
Cumbria debut
21 October 1986, v. Australians at Barrow
Cumbria caps
1, 1986
Test caps
3
Clubs
Swinton, Halifax, Widnes, Dewsbury

If there is a Rugby League gene, Les Holliday must have had it. His grandfather was Billy Little, the great Edwardian full-back for Halifax, Cumberland and England. His father was the Cumberland and Great Britain captain, Bill Holliday and Les's brother Mike also played professionally. Small wonder he appeared to be a natural footballer.

Les was one of the last of a dying breed, the specialist loose-forward, the kind of intelligent player, whose sleight of hand, telling breaks or kicking skills could make all the difference between winning and losing.

He was born in Whitehaven but played no club football in Cumbria. He played as an amateur for Folly Lane in Swinton and joined the Swinton club, making a try-scoring debut in a 43-0 victory over Doncaster in 1982. In 1984/85 he helped Swinton to the Second Division Championship, although they were immediately relegated. He had five years as a Lion, which culminated in captaining them to a 27-10 victory over Hunslet at Old Trafford in the Second Division Premiership final in 1987.

A transfer to Halifax saw him appearing at Wembley in 1988 against Wigan but he was carried off injured after 20 minutes, when neither side had scored. Without Les, Halifax crumbled to a 12-32 defeat. In 1990 he landed four goals for Halifax in the Regal Trophy final but Wigan again beat them 24-12. After scoring 152 points in 59 games for Halifax he was transferred to Widnes for £110,000 in 1990.

In his sixth game he picked up a Premiership winner's medal, scoring a try in Widnes' 28-6 beating of Bradford Northern at Old Trafford. A Charity Shield winner's medal was next in his collection, Wigan being downed 24-8 at Swansea. A Lancashire Cup winner's medal quickly followed, Salford being defeated 24-18 in the 1990 final at Wigan. The 1991/92 season brought him a try and a drop goal as Widnes hammered Leeds 24-0 in the Regal Trophy final.

Les played the 1993/94 and 1994/95 seasons for Dewsbury, setting a club record on 11 September 1994, when he scored 32 points (ten goals, two tries) in a 76-8 thrashing of Barrow. His final port of call was a return to Swinton, where he played two more years before retiring, having made 185 appearances and scored 197 points in his two spells for the Lions.

Les was unlucky not to receive more representative honours than he did. He played just once for Cumbria, scoring a try against the Australians at Barrow in 1986. He won three caps for Great Britain in 1991 and 1992, all in big victories over France. In 1990 he was selected to tour Papua and New Zealand but withdrew for personal reasons. In 1992 he did tour Australasia but an Achilles injury ended his involvement after only three games, against Canberra, Illawarra and New South Wales Country.

Tom Holliday

Winger

First-class debut
28 August 1926, Oldham v. Leeds (home)
Last game
19 January 1929, Oldham v. Widnes (away)
Cumberland debut
8 January 1927,
v. New Zealanders at Workington
Cumberland caps
7, 1927-28
England caps
1
Club
Oldham

Tom Holliday was born in Aspatria in 1898 and became famous as a Rugby Union full-back for his local club. He was so successful that in 1923 he won his first cap for England against Scotland at Inverleith. For both sides the Triple Crown, the International Championship and, of course, the Calcutta Cup were at stake. Tom pulled off a match-saving tackle on Eric Liddell, of *Chariots of Fire* fame, and England won 8-6. Tom also played in the game against France in Paris, which was won 12-3 to give England the Grand Slam.

Five more caps followed in the next three years and he went on the British Isles tour of South Africa in 1924, only to suffer a severe injury in the opening game against Western Province, which ended his participation. Earlier in 1924 he had been inspirational as captain of Cumberland & Westmorland, playing at stand-off in their 14-3 victory over Kent at Carlisle in the County Championship final. He was regarded as the side's master tactician and kicked a penalty and a conversion, goal-kicking being a skill he was never

called upon to perform in his career in league.

Tom, or 'Tosh', joined Oldham in 1926 and made his debut in a 22-12 win over Leeds at centre. His versatility was to prove useful, although he would eventually settle at left-wing for Oldham. He scored the first of 33 tries for the club in his second game, a 33-15 victory at Pontypridd, and his second try in a memorable 15-10 win against the touring New Zealanders. On 19 April 1927 he scored his first hat-trick, against Leigh at Watersheddings. Less than three weeks later, on 7 May, he repeated the feat but this time it was in the Challenge Cup final at Wigan, where Oldham demolished Swinton, who had beaten them in the previous final, 26-7. He became only the third player to score a hat-trick in a Challenge Cup final and his achievement was broadcast to the nation, the BBC covering the final for the first time. Tom's performance was not emulated until 1996 by Bradford's Robbie Paul.

Although his Oldham career lasted less than three years and took in 83 games, Tom made his mark in the representative field, indicating that Rugby League would have been richer had it claimed him earlier. He was soon starring in the Cumberland team and gained a County Championship medal for 1927/28, scoring twice against both Lancashire at Whitehaven and Yorkshire at Wakefield.

On 11 January 1928 he became a dual International, when he was a try-scorer in England's 20-12 victory over Wales at Wigan. He also played in a tour trial at Rochdale on 27 February 1928.

Dick Huddart

Second-row forward

First-class debut
18 August 1956, v. Warrington (away)
Last game
27 March 1971, Whitehaven v. Swinton (home)
Cumberland debut
19 September 1956, v. Yorkshire at Whitehaven
Cumberland caps
11, 1956-63
England caps
1
Test caps
16
Clubs
Whitehaven, St Helens, St George, Dubbo

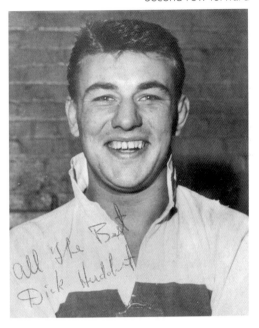

It was an up-country match in a small town in New South Wales in 1962. The pitch was bone-hard and the ground was packed to the rafters. The entire local population was there and a few more besides. The Brits were doing it tough in the early stages as the Bush footballers let them know they were in a match. Suddenly a big white-clad second-rower latched on to a cute little pass from his scrum-half, rammed his palm into a burly Bush forward's chest to send him earthwards and bolted clear of the ruck. Two defenders tried to block his path and hit the white-shirted escapee simultaneously. No one could work out exactly what they hit as they both ended up dazed in the dust.

Meanwhile the rampaging Brit had sighted the goal-line about 60 yards ahead. The Bush full-back and one of the wings should have been able to cut off a second-rower but this was no ordinary second-rower. This was Dick Huddart, 'Tiger' Huddart, 'Hurricane' Huddart, and sixty-yard tries were one of his specialities. It was tries like that which persuaded St George, the most famous club in Australia, to fork out a record £12,500 for Dick two years later.

Dick Huddart had come a long way from his native Flimby where he was born in 1936. He had played amateur rugby for Risehow and joined Whitehaven in 1955. He was a sensation from the start. In his first season he helped his club beat the touring Kangaroos 14-11, a foretaste of many defeats he would help to inflict on various Australian

opponents. He also played a huge part in taking Whitehaven to their solitary Challenge Cup semi-final in 1957, when Leeds so cruelly shattered their Wembley dream at Odsal.

A month after his debut for 'Haven he won his first cap for Cumberland, when he was one of eight Whitehaven players who shared in the 15-14 victory over Yorkshire on their own midden, the Recreation Ground. Two years later he was a test player and the hottest forward property in the game.

In 1958 Dick had become Whitehaven's first and only British Lion. He had taken Australia and New Zealand by storm. He had made his test debut at Brisbane on 5 July 1958 in one of the sport's epic matches. Britain had already lost the first test against the Aussies and the Brisbane test was do-or-die time. Huddart was one of the stars as the Lions shook off crippling injuries to win a famous 25-18 victory and then took the Ashes at Sydney with a stunning 40-17 triumph in the final test.

Dick had played in 24 of the 30 tour fixtures – more than any other tourist – and had scored 17 tries. He had also become used to playing in the very best company, thriving on the creative skills of such men as Brian McTigue, Vince Karalius and Alex Murphy.

He did not remain long at Whitehaven after the tour. St Helens lured him away and it cost them £7,250, a record sum for a forward.

Dick was in his element at St Helens, playing in a team which had all the talents and was able to use his own to maximum effect. Tackling was not his forte – others could do that. He was there to run the other team ragged. Many critics argue that the game has never seen a more devastating, damaging or explosive running forward than Dick and they may well be right. St Helens certainly got their money's worth. In five years at Knowsley Road Dick scored 76 tries in 209 appearances and won all the major domestic honours open to him.

At the end of his first season (1958/59) he collected a Championship-winner's medal, scoring a try as Saints beat Hunslet 44-22 in a magnificent final at Odsal. In 1961 Saints defeated their old enemies Wigan 12-6 at Wembley in the Challenge Cup. A summer-like afternoon gave Wembley the atmosphere of a furnace and over 95,000 fans saw a towering display from Dick Huddart, which brought him the Lance Todd Trophy. This

achievement places him in select company for the only other Cumbrians to have attained this honour are Billy Ivison (1952) and Bill Kirkbride (1970).

St Helens were one of the glamour sides of the game in Dick's time there. Apart from his Championship and Challenge Cup appearances, Dick played in four consecutive Lancashire Cup finals (1959-62), the last three of which were won. He also gained winners' medals for the Lancashire League Championship in 1959/60 and for the Western Division Championship in 1963/64.

Playing at St Helens served to place him firmly in the test selectors' spotlight. He earned a dozen test caps as a Saint, a total he may have doubled but for injuries. In 1962 he made a second Lions tour and again struck some of his finest form as Great Britain retained the Ashes. As on the 1958 tour, Dick played more games (24) than any other Lion and bagged twelve tries. He also figured in all three games Britain played in South Africa on the way home.

Dick's last test was one of the stormiest in the long history of Ashes football. By the time the third test of 1963 was played at Headingley, Britain had already lost the series. Dick had missed both previous games but was recalled for the final test in a completely restructured XIII. He was the sole Cumbrian in the team. In an absolute brute of a match – three men were dismissed – Britain upset all the odds to win 16-5 and Dick left the test scene on a high note.

A few months later he had emigrated to Australia to join St George in Sydney. In his first three seasons with them they won the Premiership, although injuries and club politics prevented him from playing in the Grand Finals of 1964 and 1965. He was, however, a major figure in their Grand Final victory over Balmain in 1966. Later he player-coached in the country with Dubbo.

In 1970/71 Cumberland had a final brief glimpse of Dick when he returned to play seven games for Whitehaven. A try tally of 126 in 358 appearances in British Rugby League was eloquent testimony to Dick's universal ranking as one of the sport's greatest attacking forwards.

First-class debut
2 September 1933,
Halifax v. Featherstone Rovers (away)
Last game
12 April 1947, Halifax v. Dewsbury (home)
Cumberland debut
18 September 1937,
v. Lancashire at Workington
Cumberland caps
6, 1937-46
England caps
4
Club
Halifax

Hudson Irving was one of the most outstanding prop forwards ever produced by Cumberland. Unfortunately he was one of that generation whose career was blighted by the Second World War. It unquestionably robbed him of a stack of county and international honours. Tragically, his life was to end on the Rugby League field, one of very few such tragedies to visit the sport.

Born in 1913 in Ellenborough, Hudson had played his schoolboy rugby in the backs. His later amateur rugby with Brookland Rovers and Flimby saw him graduate to the second row, however. It was as a second-rower that he signed for Halifax in April 1933. On his first-team debut he scored a try in a 19-9 victory at Featherstone, the first of 72 he would register for Halifax. Those 72 tries represent a club record for a Halifax forward even today. As the vast majority of Hudson's career at Halifax was as a blind-side front-rower in a period when props hardly scored, it will be realised how extraordinarily quick and mobile he was.

Aged only nineteen he was thrown in against the 1933 Australians in only his fourth first-team match and scored his side's only try in a 5-16 defeat. By the end of his first season he had also played for Halifax in a Yorkshire Cup semi-final and a Championship semi-final, as well as bagging eleven tries in 30 appearances.

Towards the end of his second season Hudson was moved to the front row and took to the work like the proverbial duck to water. At just under 5ft 11in and around 13st, he was a bit light but more than compensated with his work-rate, competitiveness, dreadnought tackling and

that priceless ability to score tries at crucial moments. He was joined at Thrum Hall by his brother George, a stand-off who was signed from Barrow. George played seven consecutive games for Cumberland (1933-35), picking up two County Championship-winners' medals in the process.

Hudson Irving had to wait until 1937 before winning his first Cumberland cap. He would win his sixth and final cap nine years later, having played in four different positions for the county, including three games on the wing. In January 1938 Hudson made his international debut for England against Wales in the first international match to be staged at Odsal Stadium.

That 1937/38 campaign saw Halifax recruiting heavily from all corners of the Rugby League world and developing into a truly formidable team. Hudson helped them to defeat the Kangaroos 12-2 at Thrum Hall but suffered the agony of a last minute 4-2 defeat by Barrow in the semi-final of the Challenge Cup. Remarkably Halifax had been forced into replays in every round preceding the semi. Their luck changed in 1938/39.

Hudson was now figuring in a team regarded as one of the best ever to have represented Halifax. It was captained by the great test loose-

Yorkshire Cup final, when Bradford Northern were triumphant at Fartown. In 1943 Hudson was again on the losing team as Halifax went down to Dewsbury 33-16 over two legs in the Championship final, although Dewsbury were later stripped of the title for fielding an ineligible player.

Victory in a wartime final finally came to Hudson and Halifax in December 1944, when Hunslet were defeated 14-3 over two legs in the Yorkshire Cup final. Halifax also reached the Championship final in 1944/45 but fell 20-26 on aggregate to arch rivals Bradford Northern. The second leg of that final at Odsal on 21 May 1945 was to be the last big game Hudson would play for the Thrum Hallers. Halifax went into decline after the war although Hudson continued to give fine service and represented Cumberland twice in the post-war period.

The 1946/47 season saw Hudson give up the Halifax captaincy but he was still a fixture in the number 10 jersey. That winter is remembered as one of the worst of the century and by April 1947 clubs were frantically trying to clear a backlog of fixtures. Halifax met Dewsbury at Thrum Hall on 12 April, their fifth game in only eight days. Hudson, now thirty-three years old, had played in all of them, including a game at Workington Town on 5 April that was abandoned at half-time, the last time he would see his native county.

In the 65th minute of the game against Dewsbury, Hudson and Halifax's Welsh hooker Bill Pritchard executed a tackle on an opposing forward. Nothing untoward happened, but Hudson never got up. He was found to be unconscious and taken quickly to the side of the field where he died within two minutes of making the tackle – apparently from a blood clot. The game was stopped immediately and so great was the shock that several of the crowd were reported to have fainted.

Ironically, a few months earlier Hudson had been granted a testimonial year by Halifax. His testimonial ultimately became a fund for his dependants, to which most of the clubs in the league contributed. Hudson Irving had been one of the most respected men ever to play for Halifax. His 391 games in the blue and white have been bettered by only a handful of players in the club's long history.

forward Harry Beverley and had a whole range of top-notchers in its ranks. Hudson enjoyed the greatest thrill in his career when he played a leading role in Halifax's 20-3 Wembley victory over Gus Risman's Salford, in the 1939 Challenge Cup final. But for the war, he would undoubtedly have shared many more triumphs.

Halifax remained one of the top teams throughout the dark days of the war and Hudson was a mainstay, captaining the club for three seasons from 1943/44 onwards. There is little doubt that he would have been a Lions tourist in 1940 but he had to be content with another three England caps against Wales and was regularly chosen for wartime representative fixtures.

The Challenge Cup was not contested in 1940, but in 1941 and 1942 Halifax reached the final to make it three consecutive appearances at the last stage. Both games were against Leeds at Odsal but both ended in defeat for Hudson Irving and his colleagues, as did the 1941

Billy Ivison
Loose-forward

First-class debut
19 September 1942,
York v Wakefield Trinity (away)
Last game
3 January 1959,
Workington Town v Swinton (away)
Cumberland debut
26 January 1946, v. Lancashire at Workington
Cumberland caps
14, 1946-57
England caps
4
Clubs
York, Workington Town

Billy Ivison was one of the most admired Rugby League forwards of the immediate post-war period. Certainly Workington Town followers would not have swapped him for any other loose-forward for he was the heart, soul and brain of the team, which brought so much sporting glory to the town and to the county, particularly in the early 1950s. Apart from the genuine genius of his play, Billy was one of the most instantly recognisable figures in the game, familiar to all through his squat, rather hunched figure and bald pate, which was sometimes obscured by the use of a scrum-cap.

His was a figure which belied his skills. The classic loose-forward was a six-footer – Billy was only 5ft 9in – and probably a good deal heavier than this favourite son of Hensingham, where he was born on 5 June 1920. Billy Ivison had all the vital ingredients to play in a Rugby League pack. He had stamina, belligerence and a willingness to work hard. What set him apart, however, was his creativity. One critic in 1952, for example, drooled over 'his judicious kicking, strong down the middle runs, defence-splitting passes and above all his priceless dummy'. Another described him simply as 'the greatest loose-forward of our time'. In short, Billy was a game-breaker, a match-winner.

Yet Billy Ivison may well have got nowhere in Rugby League. He had played a solitary game as a centre for York on 19 September 1942, scoring a try in a 28-7 defeat at Wakefield Trinity. Barrow had given him four trials in their reserve team, but decided he did not

measure up to their requirements. It was, therefore, fortuitous for Billy when Workington Town sprang into life in 1945 and gave him a chance to make good even though he had by then passed his twenty-fifth birthday. Neither party ever looked back.

Billy made his debut for Town on 6 October 1945 as a winger, scoring a try in a 15-8 home win over Liverpool Stanley. It was some time before Town realised that loose-forward was his natural position as they juggled with him as a winger, centre and stand-off. By 1947, however, he had established himself as a key member of Gus Risman's fast-developing trophy-challenging team. That team is now part of Cumbrian sporting folklore. By 1950 it had begun to earn its place in the Rugby League elite. Ivison was in the company of champion players – his pack-mates roll off the tongue even now – Hayton, McKeating, Wareing, Mudge, Thurlow and Bevan Wilson – while the backs – Risman, Lawrenson, Paskins, Gibson, George Wilson, Thomas and Pepperell – picked themselves.

In 1951 Town reached their first final when they faced Warrington at Maine Road before a crowd of over 61,000. The Rugby League Championship was the prize for the winners. History shows that Town won a spectacular

and thrilling game 26-11, cleverly exploiting a one-man advantage when Warrington lost winger Albert Johnson after only three minutes. What history tends to have forgotten is Billy Ivison's courage in playing the last half hour with a broken jaw.

If Cumbrians were ecstatic over the lifting of the Championship in 1951, their delirium was unbounded the following year when Workington Town took the Challenge Cup at Wembley with an 18-10 victory over Featherstone Rovers. Billy Ivison played the game of his life, becoming the first Cumbrian to be awarded the Lance Todd Trophy. Featherstone's captain, Eric Batten, said after the game that, 'Ivison did more than any two men to take the cup to Workington. Two of his breaks were decisive features. He is one of the most dangerous forwards I have ever played against – clever, strong, determined, fast and a tireless worker.'

By 1955 Billy had succeeded Risman as Town captain and he led them out at Wembley against Barrow in 1955. They could

not repeat their triumph of 1952, however, and went down 21-12 to their great North-Western rivals. It looked as if that Challenge Cup final was to have been Billy's finale. He was already thirty-five and did not play at all in the 1955/56 season. The retirement was premature, for he reappeared for the 1956/57 season and played on until 1959 when he made his 388th and last appearance for Town at Swinton.

There is no question that Billy Ivison was one of the all-time great loose-forwards. That fact is not reflected, however, in his representative career. Cumberland certainly knew his value, as his fourteen caps in an eleven-year county career clearly testify. At this level perhaps his most important contribution was his touchdown which beat the 1948 Australians at Whitehaven when Cumberland won 5-4.

The international selectors were for some reason less enthusiastic and failed to award him any test caps. There was particular dissatisfaction in Cumberland and in the game in general when he was overlooked for the Australasian tour of 1950. Of course, it must be remembered that there were some wonderful loose-forwards who were Billy's contemporaries – Ken Traill, Dave Valentine, Ike Owens, Harry Street and Harold Palin, to mention but a few – so the competition was intense. As Billy's skills level was not an issue, the accepted reason for his continued omission from test teams appeared to be his comparative lack of size, although many thought Town's geographical location away from the mainstream may also have contributed.

Even so Billy did play in four internationals for England (1949-52) and represented a British Empire XIII, as well as figuring in a Great Britain side which lost to France in Paris in 1952. That game was his last at the highest level. Unfortunately Great Britain v. France games at that time were not classified as tests.

Test caps aside, Billy Ivison remains one of Cumberland's enduring Rugby League legends – a magician with the ball in his hands, an inspirational figure on the pitch and one of the game's most memorable characters.

Bill Kirkbride
Second-row, prop

First-class debut
12 May 1964,
Workington Town v. Widnes (away)
Last game
23 January 1983, Rochdale Hornets v.
Wakefield Trinity (home)
Cumberland debut
12 September 1967,
v. Lancashire at Workington
Cumberland caps
7, 1967-71
Clubs
Workington Town, Halifax, Castleford,
Salford, Leigh (loan), Brisbane Souths,
Wakefield Trinity, York, Rochdale Hornets

Bill Kirkbride was born in Workington in 1944 and made his name as a professional with his local team. However, the vast majority of his long and varied career was spent well away from his native county.

A rangy second-rower at 6ft 1in and over 14st, Bill was a formidable opponent, who was unfortunate not to win more honours than he did. As an amateur playing for United Steels, he won an England Under 19 cap in a 22-6 defeat of France at Wakefield in 1963. In 1965 he graduated to become an England Under 24 International, when France were beaten 12-5 at Oldham in a stormy encounter, in which three men were dismissed.

Bill joined Workington Town at a time when they were still a force in the game but just did not have the playing or financial resources to challenge for honours. He made his debut in the last game of the 1963/64 season, playing second-row alongside Frank Foster, in an 11-10 victory at Widnes.

By 1967 he had won selection for Cumberland and must have felt at home on his debut against Lancashire at Derwent Park, for five of the pack were Town colleagues, as were four of the backs. Later that year he figured in Cumberland's great 17-15 victory over the Kangaroos at Workington. Remarkably, Bill played county rugby from four different clubs in a period of only four years.

In 1968 Bill left Town, after making 75 appearances (7 tries) to join Halifax for a fee of £6,000, another in the long line of big transfers that helped to keep Workington going. His debut against Leigh Miners Welfare in a Challenge Cup-tie on 3 February brought him the first of eight tries he would claim in 52 appearances for Halifax in a two-year stay.

Bill's next move, to Castleford for £5,750, brought his greatest recognition. Castleford were already Cup holders when they returned to Wembley in 1970 with Bill in their second-row. In the final they beat Wigan 7-2, the only try of the game stemming from Bill's charge to set up the position, from which Brian Lockwood sent over winger Alan Lowndes for the decisive score. Bill played so well that he was awarded the Lance Todd Trophy, becoming only the third, and final Cumbrian to be so honoured.

Moving to Salford for another £6,000 fee in 1971, Bill figured in their Players Trophy final defeat by Leeds at Fartown in 1973 before embarking on an even more itinerant decade which included a spell at Brisbane Souths. Most notably he was player-coach when Wakefield Trinity reached Wembley in 1979, although he did not appear in the final. His later years saw him develop into an excellent prop forward.

First-class debut
1 September 1900,
Huddersfield v. Hull KR (away)
Last game
25 March 1913,
Huddersfield v. Bradford Northern (home)
Cumberland debut
11 January 1902, v. Lancashire at Barrow
Cumberland caps
11, 1902-12
England caps
2
Club
Huddersfield

The Huddersfield 'Team of All the Talents' of the 1910-20 period was firmly ensconced in Rugby League's folklore as arguably the finest in history, at least until the Wigan team of the late 1980s and early 1990s tore up the record books. The names of the men who peopled it, trip off the tongue of anyone with an interest in the history of the game – Albert Rosenfeld, Edgar Wrigley, Ben Gronow, Stanley Moorhouse, Johnny Rogers, the great Cumbrian forward Duggie Clark, and, mightiest of all, the 'Prince of Centres', Harold Wagstaff, the immortal 'Waggy'.

Often forgotten in this pantheon is another three-quarter, who materially helped to form that iconic team – William Farrington Kitchin (sometimes spelt Kitchen). Billy Kitchin left Wath Brow, with its cramped dressing-rooms at the Greyhound Inn, for palatial Fartown in 1900. He was not joining a club that was going anywhere, except downwards. Huddersfield had not made a particularly good stab at the new Northern Union game. In his first season they finished sixth in the Yorkshire Senior Competition but were invited into an elite fourteen-club Northern Rugby League for 1901/02, finishing thirteenth. In 1902/03 the

league was split into two divisions and Huddersfield finished fifteenth out of eighteen clubs in Division One.

Billy Kitchin was obviously a top-class winger playing in a mediocre team. He was very fast, being a winner of many prizes for sprinting and had recorded 10.4 seconds for the 100 yards but was reputedly better over 220 yards. In 1902/03 he played most of his games at full-back.

Cumberland had chosen him as a winger for their clashes with Lancashire at Barrow in 1902 and at Millom in 1903, while he had figured at centre against Cheshire at Birkenhead in 1902, all the games ending in heavy defeats. By the close of the 1902/03 season Billy had left Huddersfield and decamped for South Africa, having made 83 appearances for the club, scoring 24 tries and six goals.

Things at Fartown got worse. In 1903/04 they finished bottom and were relegated to Division Two. In 1904/05 they were fifth in Division Two. Fortunately, reorganisation of the two divisions into one league for 1905/06 saved them from further decline. Coincidentally, Billy Kitchin returned from South Africa and turned out at full-back on 2 September 1905 at Dewsbury. The game was changing with county cups being inaugurated, Billy scoring a try in Huddersfield's first Yorkshire Cup-tie, a 10-9 preliminary round victory at Featherstone Rovers on 16 September 1905. He finished the season as the club's top try-scorer with nineteen. In the last ten games of the season Huddersfield only scored eleven tries, of which Billy claimed nine.

BILLY KITCHIN. The complete threequarter back and model for all youthful aspirants to football perfection. Always fit, and equally at home whether on the wing or at centre.

In 1906/07 the game changed dramatically when teams were reduced from fifteen to thirteen. The abbreviated, much faster game suited Billy down to the ground. He again top-scored with 25 tries, including five in a Cup-tie against Brighouse St James and four in league games against Wakefield Trinity and York. By now the nucleus of the great team was forming – Jim Davies, Ike Cole, Arthur Swinden, Percy Holroyd, Jack Bartholomew and the precocious Harold Wagstaff had arrived – and Billy was the senior figure.

In 1907/08 Billy was drafted into the centre to play alongside Wagstaff, scoring five tries against Batley in association with him. On 12 October 1907 he had played outside Wagstaff on the historic visit of the New Zealand All Golds to Fartown, Huddersfield losing 19-8. He was on the wing the following season when the first Kangaroos were defeated 5-3 and he set a new club record by claiming 32 tries during 1908/09.

The 1909/10 season saw him in equally good form, adding another 27 tries and being appointed captain. He made history by leading Huddersfield to their first major trophy under NU auspices. Having scored four tries against Hull KR in the first round of the Yorkshire Cup, he scored again in the final at Headingley on 27 November 1909, when Batley were demolished 21-0. In 1910 Huddersfield again reached the final only to lose 8-2 to Wakefield Trinity at

Leeds. Billy was on fire that season, topping the league's try-scorers with 41, including a club record 39. The other two tries were scored on his England debut, in a 27-8 defeat of Wales at Ebbw Vale.

Another England cap came his way in 1911, when he again scored but ended a loser, as Australia won 11-6 at Fulham. His county career had resumed in 1906, when he scored Cumberland's try in a 3-3 drawn play-off against Lancashire at Wigan, the title being shared. In 1907/08 he collected a County Championship winner's medal and played his last game in a 5-19 defeat by Yorkshire at Craven Street, Hull in 1912. He played in the centre with Jim Lomas, opposite Billy Batten and Harold Wagstaff, all captains of England, apart from Billy.

By now the Huddersfield cast was virtually complete. Billy was still holding his place as the trophy hunting accelerated. In 1911/12 the Yorkshire Cup was again won but Billy missed the final. He did, however, win Yorkshire League and League Championship medals, playing in the centre in the final at Halifax, where Wigan were beaten 13-5.

His last campaign was 1912/13, when he picked up another three winners' medals. His first try of the season on 21 September against Halifax was his 200th for the club and he finished with 211 tries and 17 goals in 296 appearances as a Fartowner.

Phil Kitchin
Stand-off

First-class debut*
19 September 1959,
Whitehaven v. Hull KR (home)
Last game
24 February 1973,
Whitehaven v. Swinton (home)
Cumberland debut
14 September 1960,
v. Yorkshire at Whitehaven
Cumberland caps
13, 1960-72
Test caps
1
Clubs
Whitehaven, Workington Town

* On 21 February, 1959 Phil Kitchin played for Kells Centre against Hunslet (away) in a first round Challenge Cup-tie

As an amateur with Kells, Phil Kitchin was very hot property. On 18 April 1959, he captained England Under 19s as a centre in an 18-8 victory over France at Wigan, having already captained Cumberland at that level and played at open age for the county. He had also twice played for England Boys Clubs against Wales at Rugby Union.

His local club Whitehaven were the fortunate winners of his signature and he made his debut in a 26-16 home defeat of Hull KR at the start of the 1959/60 season. Phil played stand-off that afternoon and he would never play any other position in a career which spanned fourteen years. Clever and creative, Phil played his entire career in Cumberland but did not play in any major finals or experience any Championship triumphs. The lack of success at club level and bad luck with injuries did not, however, mask his obvious class.

Less than a year after his Whitehaven debut, Phil turned out for Cumberland in their resounding 43-19 victory over Yorkshire at the Recreation Ground. He and Sol Roper had scintillating games against Harold Poynton and Jeff Stevenson – as good a pair of half-backs as could be imagined. Phil claimed the first of ten tries he would score in his thirteen outings for the county – an excellent strike rate, better, in fact, than his club rugby produced.

In 1965/66 Phil was in superb form. He figured prominently in Whitehaven's 12-7 victory over the New Zealanders on 2 October and won his only County Championship medal, scoring twice against Yorkshire. His greatest honour had fallen to him the previous week, when he became the first Whitehaven back to be capped at test level. He was in the Great Britain team which beat the Kiwis 7-2 at Swinton. Unfortunately, it was a truly dire game and Phil never played another test, despite his undoubted ability.

In April 1965 he had represented England Under 24s in a 17-9 success against France at Toulouse and on 5 May 1966 he had played at the Parc des Princes for a Rugby League XIII against a Paris XIII. His Cumberland career continued unabated, highlights being the 17-15 victory over the 1967 Kangaroos and captaining the side against Yorkshire in 1968 and 1970.

In February 1967, Phil was transferred to Workington for whom he played 86 games (23 tries). At Derwent Park he came close to winning trophies, Town finishing as runners-up in the Lancashire League in 1966/67, twice reaching the quarter-finals of the Top Sixteen Play-offs and losing in the Lancashire Cup semi-final to Warrington in 1967/68.

He finished his career, however, with another stint at the Recreation Ground from 1971 to 1973, bringing his career record for Whitehaven to 167 appearances, 48 tries and five goals.

Jim Lewthwaite
Winger

First-class debut
13 March 1943, *v.* St Helens (away) Cup
Last game
11 May 1957 *v.* Leeds (Wembley) Cup final
Cumberland debut
31 October, 1945 *v.* Yorkshire at Leeds
Cumberland caps
20, 1945-56
England caps
1
Club
Barrow

Jim Lewthwaite scored more tries in first-class Rugby League than any other Cumberland born player – 383 – between 1943 and 1957. Only two other Cumbrian legends have broken the 300 tries barrier – James Lomas and Ike Southward. That places Lewthwaite firmly amongst the gods.

Yet, of those 383 tries, only a dozen were claimed in Cumberland. Amazingly, he actually scored more touchdowns in Australia. The reason, of course, is because Jim Lewthwaite played his entire professional career down the coast at Barrow, a path trodden by hordes of talented Cumbrians from the north-west of the county.

Jim Lewthwaite was born in Cleator Moor in 1920. As a schoolboy he was a noted sprinter and played both soccer and Rugby Union at county level. Later he briefly played amateur Rugby League for Clifton and for Moor Row in the Cumberland League. It looked as if he was lost to Rugby League, however, when he went to work in Barrow and concentrated on soccer as a prolific-scoring centre forward with the local Crystal Palace club. Fortunately, he changed codes in 1943 and subsequently established a reputation as one of the most outstanding wingers Rugby League has seen.

His debut in a first round, first leg Challenge Cup-tie at St Helens in 1943 ended in a 2-13 defeat for Barrow but Jim was immediately picked out as a rising star. The *North-West Evening Mail* reporter was in no doubt about his potential, writing, 'He sidesteps easily, changes pace cleverly, accelerates brilliantly, and shows some of the marks which originally distinguished Alf Ellaby when he joined St Helens. With a centre to bring him out Lewthwaite might develop into something clean out of the ordinary.' To be compared to Alf Ellaby was praise indeed but the words proved prophetic.

Jim was pretty big for a winger at 6ft and around 13st. His style was direct, his creed 'get to the line as soon as possible,' and he could score from any distance. He could swerve unnervingly and possessed a devastating hand-off, allied to which he was an expert cross-kicker. He was a rare handful as an attacking force but, almost as importantly, he was a rock in defence. Just for good measure, Jim had an unsullied reputation for sportsmanship.

Jim played with Barrow in the days when they were in their pomp. Almost throughout his career with them Barrow were in the hunt for honours, played a clean and open style of rugby and nurtured a host of wonderfully gifted players. Their names are now merely echoes of halcyon days in Furness, but what memories are evoked for those they charmed

first tourist ever to score seven tries in a game, a feat which he performed in a 94-0 victory over Mackay. Only Jack Hilton in 1950 and Mick Sullivan in 1958 have emulated Jim.

At club level Jim was almost indispensable. His value to Barrow is clearly illustrated in the bare statistics of 500 appearances, 352 tries, 21 goals and 1,098 points. No one has played more games or scored more tries for the club. From 1949/50 Barrow had two of the deadliest wingers in the sport for on the left wing was the flying Frank Castle. Between them they scored over 600 tries for the club but they only appeared together once in an international. That was at Huddersfield in 1952 when Jim belatedly won his solitary England cap against the Other Nationalities. Jim scored a try that afternoon but was injured early in the second half and England succumbed 12-31.

Barrow won the Lancashire Cup in 1954 after beating Oldham 12-2 in the final at Swinton. Jim hardly missed a game in his time at Craven Park but was unfortunately injured for that red-letter day. He did, however, figure in all three of Barrow's Wembley appearances in the 1950s. He was on the right wing in 1951, when Wigan beat Barrow 10-0, and in 1957, when Leeds scraped home 9-7. His greatest triumph was reserved for the 1955 final, when Barrow defeated their Cumbrian neighbours Workington Town 21-12, an unforgettable occasion in the sporting history of the North-West.

Jim Lewthwaite defied logic and the laws of nature by becoming more prolific as his career came to its close. In 1955/56 he had posted a personal best of 41 tries for Barrow. His last season, 1956/57, during which he passed his thirty-sixth birthday, was even more productive. It began with him being awarded the captaincy of Cumberland for his last game with the county XIII, which he led to a dramatic last minute 15-14 victory over Yorkshire at Whitehaven. By the season's end he had scored 50 tries for Barrow in only 43 games, eclipsing Frank Castle's record of 47 scored in 1951/52. Jim's record stands to this day. His last game for the club – his 500th – was the Challenge Cup final at Wembley against Leeds on 11 May 1957. Barrow may have lost but Jim certainly went out in style.

– names such as Joe Jones, Bryn Knowelden, Jack Grundy, Ted Toohey, Phil Jackson, Dennis Goodwin and the man who led them, the sublime Willie Horne.

Playing in such company and with talent to burn, it was not long before Jim was winning honours. In his first season of peacetime football Jim won the first of 20 caps for Cumberland against Yorkshire at Headingley and was in such good form that he was selected for both trials, at Wigan and Leeds, for the 1946 Australasian tour. His performances were impressive and he was duly chosen to tour alongside his Barrow teammates, Horne, Knowelden and Jones.

Although Jim did not play in any of the tests, he finished as the tour's leading try-scorer with 25 tries in fifteen outings, failing to score in only three games – a magnificent achievement. Moreover, he created his own piece of Lions history when he became the

Billy Little
Scrum-half, loose-forward

First-class debut
12 March 1932,
Barrow v. Wakefield Trinity (home)
Last game
1 November 1952,
Whitehaven v. Featherstone Rovers (home)
Cumberland debut
1 October 1932, v. Yorkshire at Whitehaven
Cumberland caps
15, 1932-46
England caps
3
Clubs
Barrow, Whitehaven

Billy Little came from an avid rugby playing family. His father Joe ('Tosh') had played for Seaton RU club and Billy was one of seven brothers. Three played Rugby League for Clifton and two, Tom ('Bumley') and Joe ('Tosh', junior) played union for Workington and Cumberland in the early 1920s, being great half-backs. Billy was the youngest and certainly became the most famous.

Born in Great Clifton, he joined Workington RU club aged fifteen and was signed by Barrow, for whom he made a try-scoring debut against Wakefield Trinity in 1932. A scrum-half of solid build, there was not much Billy did not know about the tactics of that key role. He was a quick learner, too. Less than seven months after playing his first professional league game, he made another try-scoring debut for Cumberland, when Yorkshire were crushed 39-10 at Whitehaven. He went on to win County Championships with them in consecutive seasons, 1932/33 and 1933/34, and enjoyed a fourteen-year career for Cumberland.

Billy proceeded to attain international status. In 1933 he won the first of three England caps. He was in the team that defeated Other Nationalities 34-27 at Workington, while in 1934 he figured in victories against Australia at Gateshead and France in Paris, scoring tries in both games. In 1935 he was back in Paris representing a Rugby League XIII, which beat a French XIII 32-12, again being among the try-scorers. In 1936 he was selected in a tour trial at Leeds but did not make the Lions squad.

At club level his most memorable season was undoubtedly 1937/38. He picked up a Lancashire Cup runners-up medal when his side was beaten 8-4 by Warrington at Wigan, the first time Barrow had reached a major Rugby League final. A few weeks later he had the thrill of being in the Barrow team which overcame the Australians 12-8. However, his greatest moment arrived on 9 April 1938. Barrow and Halifax were locked at 2-2 in a Challenge Cup semi-final at Huddersfield as the last minute ticked away.

Billy sent Barrovians wild with delight when he picked up from a scrum, wheeled round and let fly with his left foot from forty yards and wide out. As drop goals go, it was a lulu. It sent Barrow to Wembley for the first time and concreted Billy into local folklore. At Wembley against Salford Billy dropped another, some thought even better, goal from an acute angle to level the scores at 4-4 after 65 minutes, only to see Salford snatch the cup with a last minute try.

Billy played 425 games for Barrow, scoring 47 tries and 44 goals, ending his days at Craven Park as a loose-forward. In 1948 he moved to the newly-founded Whitehaven as player-coach.

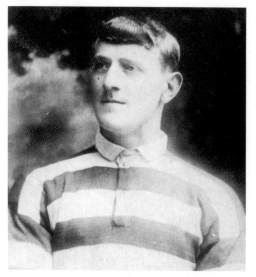

First-class debut*
20 October 1900,
Cumberland v. Lancashire at Workington
Last game
18 November 1911,
Bradford Northern v. Halifax (home)
Cumberland caps
10, 1900-09
Yorkshire caps
4, 1903
England caps
1
Clubs
Halifax, Bradford Northern

* Little's first-class debut at club level was on
21 September 1901, for Halifax at Runcorn

Billy Little was the first great Cumbrian full-back but he spent his entire first-class career in Yorkshire. He was one of the game's most famous men in the Edwardian era.

Born in Flimby in 1879, Little first played for Seaton, from where he won his first Cumberland caps in 1900. He joined Halifax in 1901 for a fee of £35 – big money for a junior player and it was an indication that Billy, a miner, knew that his talents were marketable. He was so valuable that he negotiated a deal which gave him £2 10 shillings (£2.50) per match at a time when normal winning pay at Halifax was £1 and losing money ten shillings.

Billy was paid so much because he was a genuine crowd-pleaser. He won countless games, many of them crucial cup-ties, for Halifax with his siege-gun kicking. In an era when big-kicking was an essential for full-backs few could output him and practically none would attempt goal-kicks from the range Billy bombarded the posts. The half-way line was certainly no barrier and he recorded scores of goals from over sixty yards. Colossal drop goals were another of his specialities.

Halifax won the League and Cup double in 1902/03 with Billy becoming so indispensable that for a league fixture at St Helens the club chartered a special train just for their full-back, who had to work during the morning of the match. In the Challenge Cup final at Headingley, Billy played brilliantly as Salford were defeated 7-0.

In 1903/04 Halifax retained the Challenge Cup beating Warrington 8-3 at Salford. It rounded off a season in which Billy played four times for Yorkshire and won his England cap against Other Nationalities in the first international match ever staged under Northern Union auspices.

By 1905/06, Billy elected to play again for Cumberland. In 1907/08 he played in Cumberland's victories over Lancashire, when he dropped a goal from half-way, Yorkshire and the New Zealanders. This was the first time that Cumberland had won the Championship outright.

In 1905/06 Billy captained Halifax to the first Yorkshire Cup final although Hunslet won 13-3 at Bradford. In 1907 he earned a second Championship medal, kicking three goals, as Halifax beat Oldham 18-3 at Fartown in the final. In 1908/09 he established a club record by kicking 76 goals, including three which were instrumental in beating the Australians 12-8. Halifax won both the Yorkshire League and Yorkshire Cup, three more goals, including two drops and a massive penalty, being crucial in the 9-5 victory over Hunslet in the final at Wakefield.

Billy's Halifax career ended in 1910. He had made 305 appearances, landing a record 326 goals. He was transferred to Bradford Northern for £50, retiring in 1911.

First-class debut
23 February 1952, Oldham v. Hull KR (home)
Last game
2 May 1958, Oldham v. St Helens (away)
Championship semi-final
Cumberland debut
29 September 1952, v. Yorkshire at Workington
Cumberland caps
8, 1952-56
Test caps
10
Club
Oldham

Sidney Devereux Little was one of the best second-row forwards to have played Rugby League for Cumberland.

He came to the game via a somewhat strange route, however. Born near Carlisle, Sid represented Cumberland RU and played for Harlequins. While serving at RAF stations Wittering and Cottesmore, he played for the RAF in the inter-services tournaments of 1950 and 1951, and for North-West Counties against the 1951 Springboks.

On joining Oldham he quickly made his mark as a dashing, hard-working, popular and sporting player whose second-row partnership with Welshman Charlie Winslade was as potent as any in the game. Sid's career was relatively short but it was highly successful, as Oldham developed into one of the most powerful teams of the 1950s and played in a wonderfully entertaining style.

Cumberland were quick to cap him and he made his county debut against Yorkshire at Workington in 1952, just seven months after playing his first game for Oldham. Cumberland won 8-7 but, remarkably, in his remaining seven games for the county Sid Little would never again be on the winning side.

He was on plenty of winning teams for Oldham though. His first two major finals both ended in defeat, however, in 1954/55. Sid was in the second-row when Oldham went down 12-2 to Barrow at Swinton in the Lancashire Cup final and 7-3 to Warrington at a soddened Maine Road. The 1956/57 season was a massive triumph for Oldham and Sid, who picked up three winners' medals – for the Lancashire League, for the Lancashire Cup and for the Rugby League Championship.

In 1957/58 the Lancashire League was again won, as was the Lancashire Cup, with a 13-8 victory over Wigan at Swinton before a crowd of 42,497, Sid's third appearance in the final. Oldham won the trophy for a third consecutive season in 1958/59, but Sid missed the final against St Helens.

Playing in such a successful side brought him international honours. Oddly, the selectors tended to prefer him as a blind-side prop. In October 1956 he played for Great Britain, who beat the Rest of the League 26-23 at Odsal, scoring a try. Six weeks later he made his test debut in an Ashes decider at Swinton. Australia were beaten 19-0 with Sid running in Britain's first try. He played magnificently in three tests against France later in the season, forming a brilliant front row with Alan Prescott and Tommy Harris.

Selection for Great Britain's 1957 World Cup party to Australia followed and Sid figured in all three games against France, Australia and New Zealand. The party made history by playing three games against the French in South Africa on the way home, Sid appearing in them all. His test career was rounded off in the 1957/58 season when he played in three victories against France in his normal second-row role.

James Lomas

Centre, stand-off

First-class debut*
30 September 1899,
Cumberland *v.* Cheshire at Whitehaven
Last game
29 September 1923,
Salford *v.* Wakefield Trinity (away)
Cumberland caps
14, 1899-1911
Lancashire caps
9
England caps
13
Test caps
7
Clubs
Bramley, Salford, Oldham, York

* Lomas' first-class debut at club level was on
1 September 1900, Bramley *v.* Halifax (home)

'We know him today as one of the strongest backs playing the Rugby game. We know of no man playing in the Northern Union who is so dangerous when near the line. Trained to a hair, he looks the man of muscle that he is, and with an impetuous bull-like rush he scores tries where nine out of every ten men would fail. It is to his great strength that his success as a try-getter is chiefly due, though, in saying that, one is mindful of the fact that few players are better acquainted with the tricks and artifices of the game than he.'

So wrote a Yorkshire critic of James Lomas in 1906. Lomas had been playing first-class rugby for six years at that point. He would go on for another seventeen. By 1906 he was captain of England, had broken any number of scoring records and was probably the most famous player in the Northern Union. Certainly he was the finest back Cumberland had produced in the period before the First World War and, arguably, of any period.

Jimmy, or 'Jumbo', Lomas did everything. He scored tries out of nothing and kicked shoals of goals, some of them miraculous. He played divinely at centre, half-back and full-back. His tackling was awesome, 'Observer' of The

Northern Union News writing, 'His tackling is typical of the man, and that real Cumberland "grip" has prevented many a try'. Whenever Lomas played he was the centre of attraction and he often seemed to be the man who carried the rest of his team. Yet he was no giant, standing only 5ft 7in tall and, at his heaviest, weighing a few pounds over thirteen stone.

Jimmy began his career with his native Maryport, getting into the first team at sixteen and becoming captain while still a teenager. He was a prime mover when Maryport changed from Rugby Union to the Northern Union. In 1899 he made his debut for Cumberland, char-acteristically scoring the only try of the match in a 3-0 win over Cheshire at Whitehaven.

For the 1900/01 season Jimmy signed for Bramley and finished their top scorer with 54 points. It was just a taster for what was to follow. At the start of the following season, he moved to Salford for the first £100 transfer fee and seriously began to break records. On 29 March 1902 he scored a record 31 points for Salford in a Cup-tie against Goole, more than anyone else had ever scored in the Northern Union. He later went on to bag 39 points against Liverpool City in 1907, which remains a Salford record. In 1906/07 he broke the Northern Union record by landing 86 goals and three times set or broke his own record for most points in a Northern Union season, beginning with 172 points in 1901/02, followed by 222 in 1903/04 and finally 280 in 1906/07. He led the Northern Union goal-kicking charts in 1903/04, 1906/07 and 1908/09.

By the time he finished his career at Salford, he had scored 210 tries and 465 goals in 303 games for the club. He had, however, no winners' medals to his name, despite appearances in the Challenge Cup finals of 1902, 1903 and 1906, being captain in the last two.

His trophy cabinet was, nonetheless, awash with caps. On joining Salford, he elected to play for Lancashire, making nine appearances between 1903 and 1906, including four against Cumberland. Lancashire took the title in 1903/04.

In the 1906/07 season Jimmy reverted to playing for Cumberland, going on to win fourteen caps, six of which were against Lancashire. He won two County Championships with Cumberland.

On the international front Jimmy broke much new ground. He played for England against Other Nationalities at Wigan in 1904 in the game's first international fixture. It was a twelve-a-side game but England started with only eleven as Jimmy turned up late! In the following year's fixture (played fifteen-a-side) at Bradford Park Avenue he scored his first try at this level as England won 26-11. In the 1906 fixture, the first to be played at thirteen-a-side, he was elevated to the captaincy and scored England's try in a 3-3 draw.

By 1910 he was the game's top star and was chosen to skipper the first Lions touring party to Australasia. His first test match had been at Newcastle the previous year when the Northern Union had beaten Australia 15-5, Jimmy scoring nine of the points, and he had been in charge for the final test when Australia were defeated 6-5 at Villa Park, Birmingham. The tour was hugely successful and Jimmy made a lasting impression on the Australians, who hitherto had regarded Dally Messenger as the great god of rugby, and on the New Zealanders, against whom he scored fifteen points in the only test. With 136 points in thirteen games he easily topped the tour scorers.

On returning to England Jimmy received a

benefit from Salford but then transferred to Oldham for a world record £300 fee. Ironically, he made his debut for Oldham at Salford on 4 February 1911. His career there lasted just over two years but he finally won a major domestic honour. On 6 May 1911 he was the star turn in Oldham's 20-7 Championship final victory over Wigan. The following season he picked up runners-up medals for the Challenge Cup and for the Lancashire Cup.

In 1913, in a surprise transfer, Jimmy went to York, playing for them until war ended peacetime competition in 1915. He also appeared once for York after the war and then retired. He was to have a final brief fling, however, with Salford in 1923. His career record of 535 games, 310 tries, 704 goals and 2,338 points was a truly monumental achievement.

Syd Lowdon

Utility back

First-class debut
18 August 1954, Whitehaven v. Widnes (away)
Last game
23 September 1967,
Workington Town v. Swinton (away)
Cumberland debut
15 September 1954, v. Lancashire at Wigan
Cumberland caps
20, 1954-64
Clubs
Whitehaven, Salford, Workington Town

It is doubtful that Cumberland ever produced a better all-round ball-player than Syd Lowdon, a product of Whitehaven Grammar School. As a schoolboy/youth player, he represented England at Rugby League, Rugby Union and soccer and was a gifted cricketer and tennis player. On 6 March 1954 he won an Army RU cap against the Navy, even before he had made his first-class Rugby League debut. In 1955 he again represented the Army against the RAF, partnering Barrow's test centre Phil Jackson in the centre.

Whitehaven beat off a host of competing organisations for his services and he demonstrated how good he was going to be by scoring two debut tries in a 15-13 win against Widnes. Within a month he was in the Cumberland XIII. His county debut was inauspicious, however, as he was injured and Lancashire beat the Cumbrians 24-7 at Wigan.

Syd had all the gifts – he was quick, elusive, clever – a natural athlete. He had an instinct for try-scoring and was a brilliant goal-kicker. His versatility was staggering. Whitehaven generally played him at centre but he could play anywhere from number one to number six with aplomb. One of his finest games for

Whitehaven was on the wing when he destroyed the Australians in 1956. It appeared to be all the same to Syd.

His versatility served Cumberland well in a score of county games. He played full-back, wing, centre and stand-off for Cumberland, bagging 73 points and picking up County Championship winner's medals in 1959/60, 1961/62 and 1963/64. In 1959 at Hull he scored 20 points in the 26-13 win over Yorkshire. However, he never won international honours. In 1958 he played in both tour trials but was overlooked in the final Lions selection.

After amassing 315 points in 108 games for Whitehaven, Syd was transferred for a whopping £5,250 in 1957. At The Willows he added 445 points to his tally in 72 games, rattling up 253 points in the 1958/59 season. Salford preferred to use Syd as a stand-off, although he continued to fill in almost anywhere and his last game for the club saw him grab a try and four goals from the wing against the Kangaroos. It was as a Salford player that he landed his best haul of goals – nine against both Liverpool City and Keighley in 1959.

He returned to Cumberland to play for Workington Town, scoring fifteen points on his debut, a 30-9 victory at Dewsbury on 3 October 1959. Of his 179 games for Town, 120 were as a full-back. His 548 points for Workington Town brought his career total to 1,383 in first-class football. Amazingly for such a talented player, Syd appeared in only one major final – the Western Division Championship of 1962, when Town defeated Widnes 10-0 at Wigan in a replay.

First-class debut
18 August 1958,
Workington Town v. Whitehaven (home)
Last game
3 October 1970, Whitehaven v. Swinton
(away)
Cumberland debut
27 May 1961, v. Lancashire at Salford
Cumberland caps
11, 1961-67
Test caps
1
Clubs
Workington Town, Whitehaven

Bill Martin was one of the reasons teams used to dread going to Derwent Park in the 1950s and 1960s. With forwards like him around, they knew they were in for a tough time against Workington. In the real olden days, before his time, they used to call such forwards 'dreadnoughts', men who feared no one. Bill was certainly from that school. A 6ft tall, 15st plus steelworker who usually packed down at blindside prop, Bill was a human tower of strength, immovable in the tight and an intimidating adversary. Town's great administrator Tom Mitchell wrote of him, 'In addition to being a fearsome front row man he could enrage the fans of the opposition by his "theatricals", whilst he enjoyed it all immensely'.

Unfortunately for Bill, he arrived on the scene at Workington, his local club, at the time when the great double chasing team of 1957/58 was about to break up. He made his debut in a local derby at home to Whitehaven in August 1958, which Town won 17-9. For the next seven years he was hardly ever missing and eventually put in one day less than a decade as a first-teamer.

Bill's career at Workington yielded 276 appearances and a try tally of twelve, five of which were scored in the 1962/63 season. Scoring tries was not his business! That 1962/63 season brought him his only winner's medal, when Town beat Widnes 10-0 in a replayed Western Division Championship final at Wigan.

Cumberland blooded him in their final game of the 1960/61 season. There were six Town players in the side that lost 32-18 to Lancashire and Bill probably learnt a few things from his opponent Brian McTigue. The following season he picked up a County Championship winner's medal and earned a second in 1966/67, playing his eleventh and final game for Cumberland against Yorkshire at Castleford in 1967/68.

Bill's highest honour came on 2 December 1961, when he was capped by Great Britain against France at Perpignan. Bill Drake, another Cumbrian, was the other prop.

Bill's brother Dennis, an almost equally formidable forward, played alongside him in most of his games for Workington and won seven Cumberland caps. The two played together just once for the county, however, on 12 October 1966, in an 18-14 victory over Lancashire at Warrington.

Bill played his final game for Workington on 17 August 1968 in a 17-2 home loss to Halifax. A couple of months later, 26 October, he made his debut for Whitehaven in a 22-0 beating of Batley at the Rec, going on to play 38 games for the club, scoring two tries and two goals. Dennis followed him to Whitehaven the following season, the pair helping 'Haven to reach the end of season play-offs.

Bill McAlone
Prop forward

First-class debut
19 August 1950, Whitehaven v. Oldham (home)
Last game
28 September 1960,
Whitehaven v. Leigh (home)
Cumberland debut
29 March 1954 v. Yorkshire at Whitehaven
Cumberland caps
11, 1954-59
Club
Whitehaven

Whitehaven produced some spectacularly good forwards in the 1950s, men such as John Tembey, Dick Huddart and Geoff Robinson, who eventually fetched enormous transfer fees from more affluent clubs. They went on to fame, fortune and test caps. Bill McAlone did none of those things but he was the bedrock of the packs from which those stars were hewn.

Bill was an unspectacular prop forward, who many thought was criminally underrated outside Cumberland. Whitehaven followers knew his value, however. He did the hard work uncomplainingly, bossed the front row exchanges, took whatever the opposition could throw at him and came back for more. In the scrums Bill was just about as good as it was possible to be and became known as the 'hooker-maker', any number nine playing alongside him inevitably winning the ball. At 5ft 11in and over 15st, Bill was ideally built for the job, often being described as 'Haven's 'Rock of Gibraltar'.

Before joining Whitehaven, Bill had a very short Rugby League pedigree having played just one game for Hensingham and then a few more for Kells. He made his debut, along with Billy Garratt, in the first game of the 1950/51

season, a 10-10 draw with Oldham, and he scored his first try in the last game of the season in an 18-0 home win against Barrow.

For the next ten years he scarcely missed a game. Ironically, his only significant absence from the team coincided with Whitehaven's most successful Challenge Cup run to the semi-final in 1957. Injured in a game against Oldham, he missed all four of Whitehaven's Cup-ties, Bob Vincent taking his place. Earlier in the season he had shared in Whitehaven's historic 14-11 victory over the Australians and he had scored tries in three consecutive games, a minor miracle from a player who scored just 23 in 327 games for the club.

In 1959 he appeared in the joint Whitehaven-Workington XIII which lost to the Kangaroos and later that season, 19 March 1960, he was in the team which played before Whitehaven's record crowd of 18,650 in a third round Challenge Cup-tie against Wakefield Trinity. It was Bill's try in an 11-8 victory at Leigh, the only one of the match, which got them through the second round.

Bill played county rugby in every season between 1953/54 and 1959/60. On his debut he came in for Jimmy Hayton in a play-off for the Championship against Yorkshire at Whitehaven but Cumberland lost 5-9. He had to wait until 1959 before picking up a County Championship medal, Lancashire being beaten 14-8 at Workington and Yorkshire 26-13 at Hull. It was the least he deserved.

A measure of the esteem in which Bill was held in Whitehaven was the £810 raised for his benefit in 1960. It was actually more than the great Brian Bevan had received from his benefit six years earlier.

Alan McCurrie
Hooker

First-class debut
1 January 1975,
Whitehaven v. Workington Town (away)
Last game
10 May 1987,
Whitehaven v. Swinton (away) Play-off
Cumbria debut
5 October 1977, v. Yorkshire at York
Cumbria caps
12, 1977-82
Clubs
Whitehaven, Wakefield Trinity, Oldham,
Hunslet

Odsal, 29 August 1982 – early in the game Oldham's number nine, bearded and grey-haired, although he was only about twenty-eight, picks up the ball under his own posts, dummies and breaks through the Bradford Northern line. He moves the ball on and then rejoins the move twenty yards from the home goal-line and scampers over for a try. Hookers are not supposed to do that but this was Alan McCurrie, who, apart from running in a hat-trick went on to completely dominate the game, which Oldham won 23-10.

Alan McCurrie was an extraordinary hooker, who did all the things good hookers did in the '70s and '80s – win the ball, tackle round the ruck, act as dummy-half. He did more, though, much of it outrageously unpredictable. He had the nerve to try the unexpected and it often came off, baffling opponents and delighting spectators. He scored tries almost as frequently as a good half-back and dropped goals for good measure.

Alan joined Whitehaven from Wath Brow and became a popular hero at the Recreation Ground, making his debut in a 10-3 derby victory at Workington in 1975. In 1977/78 he played in all 31 of Whitehaven's fixtures and topped the try-scorers with fifteen. At the start of the following season he scored five tries in four games, including all three in a 15-8 victory over Bramley, but was transferred to Wakefield Trinity for £10,000.

With Trinity he played at Wembley in 1979 but had to accept a runners-up medal as Widnes beat them 12-3 in a poor Challenge Cup final. Two days later he scored a hat-trick in a 23-3 win at Rochdale. In 1979/80 Trinity lost in the semi-finals of the Yorkshire Cup and John Player Trophy, the nearest he would come to playing in another major final. Between 1979 and 1981 he proved his durability by playing in 87 consecutive games. Trinity were relegated in 1981/82 but Alan had left to join Oldham who won the Second Division Championship. In his first full season, 1982/83, at Watersheddings he was an ever-present through 35 games and all told made 120 appearances for Oldham (21 tries, four drop goals).

His career ended with a season at Hunslet, followed by a return to his roots at Whitehaven, where he scored a try in a club record victory in 1986 – 72-6 against Fulham in a Lancashire Cup-tie.

Alan deserved international status but had to settle for a dozen caps for Cumbria. He made his debut in 1977 against Yorkshire and enjoyed five good years. Cumbria won the County Championship in 1980, when they also beat the New Zealanders 9-3 at Whitehaven. Alan picked up a second winner's medal in 1981, when Lancashire were beaten 27-15 at Wigan, Alan and Nicky Kiss both being sent off, and Yorkshire despatched 20-10 at Whitehaven.

Loose-forward, second-row, prop

First-class debut
4 May 1963,
Workington Town v. Castleford (away)
Last game
13 February 1977, Barrow v. York (away) Cup
Cumberland debut
16 September 1964, v. Lancashire at Blackpool
Cumberland caps
17, 1964-75
Clubs
Workington Town, Barrow, Whitehaven

Although he was a Whitehaven lad, John 'Spanky' McFarlane began his professional Rugby League as a Workington Town player but played for all three of the senior clubs in the North-West. His playing days spanned fourteen years and he made a massive 438 first-class appearances. In the process he acquired a kind of heroic status in West Cumberland as a player who never gave in, who covered every inch of the pitch in attack and defence and was the archetypal all-action Cumbrian forward. He had a neat line in dropping goals and although he was not a try-scorer of any note (37 in his career), some of his scores were genuine match-winners.

Spanky's debut was as a loose-forward in Workington's 18-7 defeat at Castleford at the close of the 1962/63 season, a campaign in which the Western Division Championship was won and the Lancashire Cup semi-final reached. While Town remained a top ten club for the next half-dozen seasons, there were no winners' medals for Spanky, just a tankard when Town won the fifth period of the Mackeson Trophy for points scoring in 1963/64.

After eight years, in which he played 212 games and scored 20 tries and 14 goals for Town, Spanky transferred to Barrow, making his debut in the second row alongside Frank Foster at Salford on Boxing Day 1969. He remained at Craven Park until 1971 (52 games,

two tries, two goals) before being sold to Whitehaven for a club record fee of £3,000.

Spanky made his first appearance for 'Haven in a 30-9 home victory over Hunslet on 4 September 1971 and immediately became an icon at the Recreation Ground. In 1972/73 he captained them in a campaign which brought First Division status to Whitehaven. In subsequent seasons he skippered Whitehaven to the semi-finals of the Lancashire Cup and the John Player Trophy – big achievements for a small town club. By the time he played his 137th and last game (13 tries, 28 goals) for Whitehaven against Blackpool on 23 January 1976, Spanky had gravitated to prop. His career ended with another twenty games for Barrow.

A splendid seventeen-cap career for Cumberland began at Blackpool in 1964, where a famous 13-11 victory over Lancashire was recorded. He played loose-forward on that occasion, but also represented Cumberland at second-row and blind-side prop. The following season he figured in a 19-3 win against Yorkshire at Craven Park, Hull, which helped bring the County Championship to Cumberland. There was disappointment in 1973, however, when Yorkshire beat Cumberland 20-7 in a play-off for the title at Leeds, and when the Australians overpowered the Cumbrians 28-2 at Whitehaven.

By the time he played his last games, Cumberland had transmogrified into Cumbria and in December 1975 Spanky had the distinction of captaining the team against Lancashire (lost 22-17) and Other Nationalities (won 21-13).

Danny McKeating
Hooker

First-class debut
26 March 1932, Barrow v. Leigh (home)
Last game
7 October 1944, Barrow v. Oldham (home)
Cumberland debut
29 September 1934, v. Yorkshire at Whitehaven
Cumberland caps
8, 1934-37
Club
Barrow

Danny McKeating was born in Workington and played amateur rugby for Seaton. His father was a forward with Dearham Wanderers and his younger brother Vincent was one of the best hookers of the immediate post-war years. Hooking appeared to be in the McKeating genes, for many critics thought that Danny had few superiors in that dark art when he played for Barrow in the 1930s.

Barrow signed Danny on 20 August 1932 but he had already made his first-team debut against Leigh the previous March. For the remainder of the decade Danny would be almost inseparable from the Barrow number nine jersey. Ideally built for a hooker at 5ft 8in and 12st 7lbs, Danny ensured that Barrow were never short of the ball, as they gradually built up a team which could challenge for honours.

It took Danny 71 games to score his first try for Barrow, against St Helens who were beaten 21-10 at Craven Park on 31 March 1934. In 301 appearances for the club he would only claim thirteen tries – par for the course for a hooker in those times. Perhaps his most crucial try was his match-winner in a 3-0 victory over Streatham & Mitcham on 5 December 1936.

The 1936/37 season gave Danny and Barrow their first sniff of trophy success when they reached the semi-final of the Lancashire Cup, only to lose 13-19 at home to Salford, after a 15-15 draw at The Willows. The following season, however, saw Barrow go one better as they reached the Lancashire Cup final for the first time. There was anti-climax, however, as Warrington beat them 8-4 at Wigan.

Later that season Barrow suffered defeat in the Championship semi-final at Hunslet but

qualified for a first Wembley appearance on 7 May 1938. Their Cup final opponents were Salford and again there was a runners-up medal for Danny, as Salford scored a last minute try to win the Challenge Cup 7-4. With skipper Alec Troup injured in the first few minutes, Danny performed miraculously in the scrums to outhook Welsh International Bert Day 50-26, which probably kept the score-line to such reasonable proportions.

At county level Danny would have won far more than eight Cumberland caps had the Second World War not intervened. Propped by Stan Satterthwaite (Leeds) and Joe Wright (Swinton), Cumberland had a sure-fire ball-winning machine in the years of Danny's hooking occupancy. His first season, 1934/35, brought him a County Championship winner's medal, as Yorkshire were beaten 10-0 at Whitehaven and Lancashire 15-5 on his home ground at Barrow.

Surprisingly, Danny never won an international cap. The nearest he came was on 1 November 1937, when he represented a star-studded British Empire XIII that beat France 15-0 in Paris, thereby winning the Paris Exhibition Cup. His winning pay was £6.

Vince McKeating

Hooker

First-class debut
10 March 1945,
Leeds v. Featherstone Rovers (away)
Last game
1 December 1956, Barrow v. Leeds (home)
Cumberland debut
26 January 1946, v. Lancashire at Workington
Cumberland caps
9, 1946-54
England caps
2
Test caps
2
Clubs
Leeds (guest), Dewsbury, Workington Town,
Barrow

Like his brother Danny, Vince McKeating was born in Workington but played his junior Rugby League for Risedale Old Boys in Barrow.

His first senior game was as a guest for Leeds in a 12-5 victory at Featherstone in 1945. However, it was for Dewsbury that he signed professional forms, making his debut in a 20-11 home win against Bramley on 1 September 1945. With Dewsbury he gained a reputation as one of the game's best ball-winners and he played a big part in getting them to the Championship final of 1947, landing the first of only two career goals in the 5-2 semi-final defeat of Widnes. In the final he matched Joe Egan in the scrums but Wigan won 13-4. Dewsbury did, however, lift the 1946/47 Yorkshire League Championship.

After playing 117 games for Dewsbury, Vince returned to Cumberland, making his debut for Workington Town at Belle Vue Rangers on 21 August 1948. Amazingly, he did not miss a game during his first three seasons with Town, putting together a run of 145 consecutive club appearances, including four for Dewsbury, between 1948 and 1951. The sequence was ended by his selection for the first test against New Zealand on 6 October 1951, which Great Britain won 21-15 at Bradford. Vince also played, and scored a rare try, in the second test

victory at Swinton, the first ever to be televised.

His stay at Workington brought him 206 appearances for the club, including the Championship final of 1951, when Warrington were beaten 26-11 at Maine Road. He also contributed mightily to Town's victory over Featherstone Rovers at Wembley in 1952.

In 1953 Vince moved down the coast to Barrow for the paltry fee of £200. He proved he was far from finished by making another 120 appearances for the club. In 1954/55 he starred in Barrow's greatest season, collecting a Lancashire Cup winner's medal, when Oldham were beaten 12-2 in the final at Swinton. He then put in a wonderful performance in the 1955 Challenge Cup final against his former club Workington, who were beaten 21-12. Vince mopped up the scrums 50-26 and scored the first try of the game, albeit from a dubious forward pass. The following season he helped Barrow defeat the New Zealanders 17-15 and played in losing semi-finals in both the Lancashire and Challenge Cups.

For a hooker Vince was exceptionally big, topping 6ft and eventually weighing over 14st, but few rivals could stop him winning scrums. Besides his Great Britain caps, Vince was also capped by England against Wales at St Helens and France at Marseille in 1951 and made a two-match tour of France with a British Empire team in May 1949. His Cumberland career brought him a County Championship winner's medal in 1948/49.

John McKeown

First-class debut
21 August 1948, Whitehaven v. Hull (home)
Last game
11 November 1961,
Whitehaven v. Rochdale Hornets (away)
Cumberland debut
12 October 1949, v. Lancashire at Workington
Cumberland caps
15, 1949-60
International caps*
1
Club
Whitehaven

* McKeown's appearance for Great Britain was not a test match. It was classed as an international

As a maker and breaker of records John James McKeown rates among the most prolific of all Cumbrian players.

John McKeown joined Whitehaven from Risehow in 1948, when the club was formed. He played his entire career at Whitehaven and is one of the club's enduring legends.

As a goal-kicker Whitehaven will probably never see his equal and as a full-back his qualities were well described by Walter Thomson of the *Whitehaven News* in 1956, 'Remorseless in defence, impeccable in fielding, astute in touch-finding, and, at times, devastating in linking up, McKeown may not be the fastest full-back playing football but he wouldn't be boasting to call himself the best all-rounder'.

Mac made his debut in Whitehaven's inaugural game against Hull at the Recreation Ground in 1948. The game was won 5-0 and, oddly enough, the full-back failed to score. In the next game at Batley he kicked the first of a record 1,050 points that he landed for the club over the next thirteen years.

In 1953/54 he booted a record 105 goals for 'Haven, extended the record to 120 in 1955/56 and to 141 in 1956/57. That figure remains a record to this day. He also passed the century mark in 1957/58 and 1959/60. His best haul in a game was nine against York in a 51-12 rout at the Rec on 16 August 1958.

In his second season John made his debut for Cumberland in a 22-11 success against Lancashire at Workington. He was the only Whitehaven player in the team and again on his first appearance he did not kick a goal, Jeff Bawden landing five. He made up for it though, landing 39 for the county in the next eleven years and coming close to Billy Holding's career record of 45 goals. In his last appearance for Cumberland on 14 September 1960, he set a county record by kicking eight goals in a 43-19 drubbing of Yorkshire, fittingly enough, on his home ground.

John again made history on 11 April 1956, when he became Whitehaven's first international player. When Glyn Moses was withdrawn to play for St Helens in a Challenge Cup semi-final replay, Mac was drafted into the Great Britain team that beat France 18-10 in a floodlit match at Bradford. The full-back contributed three goals to the victory.

There were no domestic honours for Whitehaven and John in his long career but he did figure in all the club's big occasions – a 14-11 victory over Clive Churchill's Aussies in 1956, the run to the Challenge Cup semi-final in 1957, the record crowd (18,650) at the Rec in the Cup against Wakefield Trinity in 1960, and, of course, all those occasions when his skill with the boot meant the difference between victory and defeat.

First-class debut
11 September 1897,
Wakefield Trinity v. Manningham (away)
Last game
22 April 1911, Wakefield Trinity v. Oldham
(away) Championship semi-final
Yorkshire caps (NU)
4, 1897-99
Yorkshire caps (RU)
7

Club
Wakefield Trinity

Full-back Jimmy Metcalfe was one of the most famous Cumbrian players of the early Northern Union period – in Yorkshire!

He began his rugby career with Askam in the early 1890s but then migrated to Barnsley and ended up playing for Featherstone (not the Rovers), who were runners-up to Hull KR in the Yorkshire RU First Competition in 1896/97. That was a bumper season for Jimmy. He played in all seven of Yorkshire's fixtures, only one of which was lost – ironically, the game against Cumberland at Castleford. He also came very near to an England cap, figuring in both North versus South trials, at Richmond and Dewsbury.

A critic wrote of Jimmy, 'He is a real gem of a full-back, who is cool and collected as any veteran and can kick about twice as far as the average. Metcalfe has the ability to astonish both spectators and defences alike'. He was a master in the three pre-requisites of full-back play in his era – tackling, fielding and kicking. Try-scoring was not considered a full-back's province and Jimmy obviously agreed, scoring

only three in almost 400 first-class NU games.

In 1897/98 he joined Wakefield Trinity, with whom he would remain until retiring in 1911. For most of that period Trinity never rose above mediocrity but Jimmy was a beacon at the back, consistent and safe as houses. He landed the first of 389 goals for Trinity at Liversedge on 4 December 1897, and went on to establish a number of records. On 8 March 1902, he landed a record nine goals in a 36-0 home victory over Liversedge, the last of which made him the first Trinity player to amass 50 goals in a NU season, 51 being his season's tally. He broke both records again in 1908/09 when he booted 65 goals, including eleven in a 67-10 drubbing of Bramley.

On 6 November 1897, he won the first of four county caps for Yorkshire under NU laws in a 22-3 victory over Cheshire at Stockport. In 1898/99 he was full-back in all of Yorkshire's successful games against Cheshire, Lancashire and Cumberland. Yorkshire won the County Championship in both his seasons with them.

Trinity developed into a power in the latter part of his career at Belle Vue. He played in their drawn game against the 1907 New Zealanders and in 1908 he kicked four goals in a 20-13 beating of the Australians. In 1909/10 and 1910/11 he earned Yorkshire League Championship medals and was in the team that beat Huddersfield 8-2 at Headingley in the Yorkshire Cup final of 1910, landing a first-minute penalty goal. His most prestigious medal, however, was gained on 24 April 1909, again at Headingley, when Wakefield overpowered Hull 17-0 in the Challenge Cup final.

First-class debut
18 November 1929, Salford v. Swinton (away)
Lancashire Cup semi-final
Last game
22 December 1945,
Salford v. Broughton Rangers (away)
Cumberland debut
20 September 1930, v. Yorkshire at Whitehaven
Cumberland caps
18, 1930-38
Clubs
Salford; Dewsbury and Leeds (wartime guest)

When someone as distinguished as Gus Risman says that a player is the best utility back he has played with, then that player must have been pretty damn good. Risman said that about Sammy Miller.

Sammy was born in Aspatria but made his name playing Rugby Union for Blaydon and Northumberland before signing for Salford in 1929. He joined a team that would develop into one of the best in the game's history with Risman as its captain and Lance Todd as its manager. Sammy could play anywhere in the backs, although centre was his usual position, where he played most of his biggest games. He was apparently a skilled wrestler, which might have helped to account for the fact that he was 'wonderfully good in defence'. He was quick enough in attack to make the initial break and hardly ever played a bad game.

He made a dramatic debut at stand-off for Salford in a replayed Lancashire Cup semi-final against arch-rivals Swinton, which ended scoreless. Salford won the second replay and Sammy's third game was the Lancashire Cup final. Unfortunately, Salford lost 15-2 to Warrington at Wigan but it was just the prelude to the most successful period in the club's history.

Sammy played all over the place before settling at centre in the 1932/33 season. He won five Lancashire League Championship medals – 1932/33, 1933/34, 1934/35, 1936/37 and 1938/39. He also played in six Lancashire Cup finals, taking winner's medals in 1931, 1934, 1935 and 1936. He played in three Championship finals for Salford, being a winner in 1933 against Swinton and 1939

against Castleford, playing at full-back in the latter final at Maine Road. In 1938 he was left out of Salford's Challenge Cup-winning side against Barrow but played at Wembley in 1939, when a 'flu-troubled Salford lost heavily to Halifax.

In 1934 Sammy was a member of the Salford squad that toured France and were immortalised as the Red Devils (*les diables rouges*).

Salford closed down in 1941 and Sammy had a season with the great Dewsbury side in 1941/42, helping them to lift the Championship with a 13-0 victory over Bradford Northern in the final at Leeds. Five of the Dewsbury backs were Salford players on wartime guest loan arrangements. He made 25 appearances for Dewsbury (7 tries, 6 goals) to add to the 312 games he played for Salford (81 tries, 57 goals). He also played as a guest once for Leeds in 1942. Sammy was a useful kicker, landing eight against Bradford in 1930 and nine in the last pre-war game against Rochdale in 1939.

His Cumberland career tested his versatility for he played centre, stand-off, scrum-half and wing for the county in his eighteen appearances. He was a member of the County Championship-winning sides of 1932/33, 1933/34 and 1934/35.

Bob Nicholson

Second-row, prop

First-class debut
7 October 1944, Huddersfield v. Wigan (away)
Last game
15 August 1952, Whitehaven v. Widnes (home)
Cumberland debut
31 October 1945, v. Yorkshire at Leeds
Cumberland caps
11, 1945-51
England caps
7
Test caps
3
Clubs
Huddersfield, Whitehaven

One of the most outstanding second-rowers of the immediate post-war period, Bob Nicholson was born in Dearham in 1921 and was a product of the Hensingham club.

He was signed by Huddersfield on 21 March 1939 but did not play a first-team game until 1944 because of the war and his duties with the RAF. By the start of the 1945/46 season Bob had just three first-team appearances to his credit. By the close of the season he still only had 21 first-team games behind him but had played for a British RL XIII in Paris, scoring a try in a 19-6 victory over France. He had also been capped by Cumberland and England and had won a place on the 1946 Lions tour. He was making up for lost time.

His first season had also seen him win a runners-up medal for the League Championship, although he missed the final against Wigan as he was en route to Australasia.

The tour was like the curate's egg for Bob. After playing in the opening fixture, scoring a try against Southern Districts at Junee, he contracted a chest infection, which prevented him from playing in the next thirteen games and kept him out of the entire Ashes series. He did, however, play in six of the seven fixtures

in New Zealand, making his test debut in the only test against the Kiwis at Auckland.

Bob was extremely quick, good in the scrums, a relentless support player and a man with a penchant for scoring tries. In 1947/48 he scored 16 tries for Huddersfield, having played over half the season at prop. He actually bagged a hat-trick playing blind-side prop against Castleford, a rare occurrence.

The 1948/49 season could fairly be described as his most momentous. Bob played in four victorious games against the Kangaroos – for Huddersfield who beat them 22-3, for Cumberland who won 5-4 at Whitehaven, and in the first and second tests at Headingley (23-21) and Swinton (16-7). Illness kept him out of the third test. To round off a glorious campaign, he was in the Huddersfield team that beat Warrington 13-12 in a magnificent Championship final at Maine Road. He also earned a Yorkshire League Championship medal.

In 1949/50 he won another Yorkshire League Championship medal but had to settle for runners-up medals from the Yorkshire Cup final and the Championship final. In 1950/51 he figured in his last major event – the 18-9 Yorkshire Cup final victory over Castleford. He played his 180th and last game (46 tries, 2 goals) for the Fartowners on 28 April 1951 in a 38-6 home drubbing of Hull KR.

He wound down his career with a year at Whitehaven (36 games, 7 tries, 6 goals), becoming a publican and a director of the club.

Sammy Northmore
Half-back

Northern Union debut*
4 September 1897, Millom v. Barton (home)
Last first class game
Unknown, but probably for Millom in the 1901/02 season
Cumberland debut
19 November 1898, v. Cheshire at Runcorn
Cumberland caps
5, 1898-99
England caps (RU)
1
Club
Millom

* Northmore's first class NU debut was on 26 February 1898, for Millom v. Salford (away) Cup

Sammy Northmore was a native of Millom, although his parents originated in Devon, and a product of the Millom RU club, which converted to the Northern Union in 1897.

Before playing Northern Union Sammy had a distinguished career as a half-back in Rugby Union. He was capped by Cumberland and in 1897 won a place in the North v. South trial at Dewsbury, which the North won. Also in the North XV were four fellow Cumbrians – Jimmy Metcalfe at full-back and three members of the pack, Millom's Edward Knowles and Sam Hoggarth and Aspatria's James Davidson. Sammy played well enough to win a place in the England team, which lost 13-9 to Ireland in Dublin on 6 February 1897. Sammy's last big game under Rugby Union laws was the final of the County Championship, when Cumberland lost 3-9 to Kent at Carlisle on 10 April 1897.

For the 1894/95 season Sammy abandoned Millom and joined their rivals in the North-Western League, Barrow. He was outstanding in a memorable season. Barrow won the North-Western League, ironically with Millom runners-up. They also won the more prestigious Lancashire Second Class Club Championship, Sammy grabbing the only try of the game at Widnes on 23 March 1895, which effectively won the trophy.

The local Barrow paper described him, 'This clever half-back is famous for his brilliant strategy in eluding opponents, which enables him to 'pass' with great rapidity and accuracy'.

At only 5ft 6in and 10st 5lbs, he needed to be quick on his feet and between the ears.

Returning to Millom, Sammy became the first captain of the Cumberland NU team, taking part in all the historic opening games. A non-championship game was arranged for 5 February 1898 against Yorkshire at Hunslet, Sammy leading a XV containing twelve Millom players. The game was lost 8-0 but Cumberland county NU rugby had been successfully launched. The first championship match followed on 19 November, when Cumberland lost 4-3 to Cheshire at Runcorn. On 3 December 1898, Sammy led his team to their first victory, Lancashire being their victims by 13-3 at Workington.

Later that season he led Millom to the Lancashire Second Competition Championship and, in a 'test match' play-off at Salford on 26 April 1899, they defeated Morecambe, who had finished bottom of the Lancashire Senior Competition, by 11-0, Sammy scoring the first try. Millom thus won promotion to the LSC.

In 1899 Sammy played his last two games for Cumberland, forming an intriguing half-back partnership with Maryport's rising star Jim Lomas. He led the county to a 3-0 victory over Cheshire at Whitehaven and ended his county career against Yorkshire on 25 November 1899, most appropriately, on Millom's home ground, Salthouse.

First-class debut
10 March 1923, Huddersfield v. Keighley (away)
Last game
7 April 1945, Hull v. Dewsbury (away)
Cumberland debut
17 October 1923, v. Yorkshire at Hunslet
Cumberland caps
35, 1923-37
England caps
4
Test caps
4
Clubs
Huddersfield, Batley, Hull, Hull KR

Joe Oliver hailed from Maryport. At fifteen he was playing for Glasson Rangers but then had a dalliance with soccer at Flimby before returning to Rugby League. Huddersfield, a club with a decided knack of spotting Cumbrian talent, persuaded him to turn professional in 1923. In those days Joe was a full-back, turning out in that position for his debut in a 15-0 victory at Keighley, when he kicked a couple of goals. They would be the first in a torrent.

Joe had a difficult act to follow at Fartown. Harold Wagstaff, 'the Prince of Centres', was still holding the reins but his glorious 'Team of all the Talents' had all but broken up. Joe himself was more than adequately filling the boots of Gwyn Thomas, one of the finest full-backs the game had seen. Joe remained at Huddersfield for just short of four years, helping them to the Yorkshire Cup finals of 1923, 1925 and 1926, picking up a winner's medal for the last, when Wakefield Trinity were beaten 10-3 at Headingley.

Huddersfield had decided to play Joe at centre in the 1925/26 season. They were rewarded well as he ran in 21 tries, including his first hat-trick, ironically enough in a Challenge Cup-tie in Cumberland against Hensingham on 13 February 1926, when the locals were beaten 33-0. In January 1927, however, Joe was transferred to Batley for £300. He had played 113 games as a Fartowner, scoring 232 points.

Joe made his Batley debut in a 2-0 defeat at Hunslet on 29 January 1927. Batley alternated

him between full-back and centre but the representative selectors clearly saw him as a top-notch centre. Cumberland had been playing him in that position since 1923 and in 1928 he was selected to play for England against Wales at right centre to the legendary winger Alf Ellaby. The game at Wigan on 11 January was a triumph for Joe. He scored a try, helped Ellaby to a hat-trick and England won 20-12. Six weeks later Joe was chosen to play in the second tour trial at Rochdale and was subsequently selected to tour Australasia as a centre in the summer of 1928.

On tour Joe played in only nine of the 24 games as injury played havoc with the tourists' centre-three-quarters. Swinton's Jack Evans played three matches and Leeds' Mel Rosser only matched Joe's total. The only centre to escape injuries was Joe's fellow Cumbrian Jim Brough (Leeds). Nevertheless, Joe proved a key figure in the Ashes-winning series, figuring in all three tests as well as in the first test in New Zealand.

Shortly after his return from the tour, Joe moved from Batley to Hull for a massive £550. His debut, a 10-4 home defeat by St Helens, in which he landed two goals on 27 October 1928, marked the beginning of a long-running love affair with Humberside. He became the idol of The Boulevard. Hull dispensed with any idea of playing him anywhere but centre and made him their first choice goal-kicker – he had only kicked 19 goals in 57 games for Batley.

For the next ten years, several spent as captain, Joe Oliver enthralled the Hull faithful.

Joe Oliver's 1935-36 Hull team that won the Championship and Yorkshire League.

He was a rare handful – heavy, aggressive, powerful and with an eye for the gap. His surging charges down the centre of the field became part of the game's folklore and the greatest compliment to his popularity was the Hull fans' acceptance of him as the natural successor to their own immortal Billy Batten. By 1938 he had won countless games for his side with 1,769 points (153 tries, 655 goals) in 379 appearances. He had also won another three caps for England against Australia, Wales and France.

In 1935/36 Joe led Hull to the Yorkshire League Championship and to the Rugby League Championship, his most successful season in domestic football. The Championship final against Widnes at Fartown on 9 May saw him play one of the games of his life. At half-time the teams were level at 2-2, Joe having contributed a penalty goal. In the second half, however, he ran Widnes ragged as Hull finished 21-2 winners. Joe ended up with 16 points (two tries, five goals) and was chaired from the field at the close. His second try, a diagonal run, was described as 'a masterpiece'.

In March 1938 Joe crossed the city to play for Hull KR. His 34th and last game for the Rovers was a 7-3 home win over Leigh on 25 February 1939. Ostensibly it was the end of a magnificent career especially as the Second World War followed fairly rapidly. Four years later, however, Joe emerged from retirement to play for Hull again. Remarkably he played all 26 games for Hull in 1943/44 and a further 21 in 1944/45. Joe thus brought his career figures for Hull to 426 appearances, in which he amassed 1,842 points. Mercifully perhaps, these last two seasons saw him restored to full-back.

Joe Oliver's claim to greatness is enhanced when his county career is examined. Quite simply, no one has ever played as many games for Cumberland as Joe's 35 which, astonishingly, were played consecutively between 1923 and 1937. Typically he broke the record (31 appearances jointly held by Joe Ferguson and Douglas Clark) with a match-winning two-try performance against Yorkshire at Workington on 10 October 1936. Joe's 99 points for Cumberland is also a record.

Joe Oliver's final career record reads: 679 appearances, 217 tries, 841 goals and 2,333 points. In any terms those statistics are staggering.

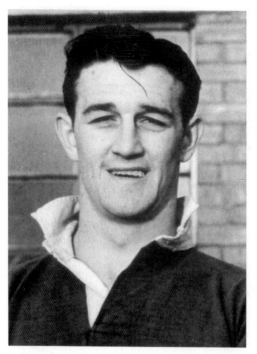

First-class debut
1 September 1956, Workington Town v.
Salford (away) Lancashire Cup
Last game
19 March 1966,
Workington Town v. Hull KR (home) Cup
Cumberland debut
15 September 1958, v. Yorkshire at Whitehaven
Cumberland caps
14, 1958-64
Club
Workington Town

John O'Neill cut a striking figure. At 6ft 1in and eventually topping 14st, his gangling frame was surprisingly deceptive, for he had a neat side-step, was a natural but sometimes unorthodox footballer, who ran very upright with a high knee action and did not shirk his defensive duties. Some critics likened him to his great contemporary Wigan's Eric Ashton, which was high praise.

Although local boy John earned his reputation with Workington Town as a prolific try-scoring centre, he had represented England amateurs at Under-21 level as a second-rower against France at Tarbes on 15 April 1956 in a 10-8 victory. Town were quickly in for his services and he made his debut five months later at left centre, as partner to Bill Wookey, in a 9-17 defeat at Salford in a first round Lancashire Cup-tie. A week later he scored the first of 117 tries for the club in a 15-9 win at Wakefield Trinity. He played 271 games for Workington.

In 1957/58 he had a superb season as Town reached Wembley, had a run of 22 unbeaten matches and contested the Championship final. His form at right centre to Ike Southward was a revelation. John claimed 20 tries in 41 games

and played in both finals, only to experience defeat against Wigan and Hull.

John played in an era of outstanding centres, having to contend with the likes of Neil Fox, Alan Davies, Jim Challinor, Eric Ashton and Phil Jackson, to name but a few. In other circumstances he may have been a test man. Instead he had to be content with fourteen Cumberland caps, beginning with a 29-7 win over Yorkshire at Whitehaven in 1958, when he showed up well against a young Neil Fox. On 14 September 1960, again against Yorkshire at the Rec, he wrote himself into county history. Partnered in the centre by Dick Huddart, Cumberland hammered their more illustrious opponents 43-19 and John equalled Jack Coulson's county record of four tries set back in 1932. No one has since emulated the feat.

John's Cumberland career brought him County Championship winner's medals in 1961/62 and 1963/64, while his ten career tries for the county have seldom been exceeded. Cumberland's performance against Yorkshire in 1960 came at a very opportune time because the Rugby League was seriously considering dropping Cumberland from the County Championship and replacing them with an 'Other Counties' team.

The season continued to be a good one for John who led Town's scorers with 21 tries. He did even better in 1962/63 with 24 tries from 40 games, including three in a 27-9 victory over Wigan in the semi-final of the Western Division Championship. He went on to pick up his only winner's medal when Widnes were beaten in the final.

First-class debut
17 October 1899, Oldham v. Stockport (home)
Last game
15 February 1913, Oldham v. Widnes (away)
Cumberland debut
15 October 1904, v. Cheshire at Birkenhead
Cumberland caps
18, 1904-11
Club
Oldham

Joe Owens was a tough bugger. At least that is what they said around Oldham for years. Joe had once played for the Roughyeds against Swinton with a broken hand when the team was strapped for numbers. He had been retired from the game for several years, when he was reported missing in action, presumably killed, in the Gallipoli campaign in Turkey during the First World War. It therefore came as a great surprise when Oldham were preparing in the dressing-room at Leeds and there was a knock at the door. In hobbled Joe on crutches, wounded but very much alive, asking if they were a player short!

Joe had been signed in 1899 from Seaton, having previously played with Payhouse Rangers. He was a winger at the time but played most of his professional career in the pack. His debut for Oldham, a 19-5 victory over Stockport, saw him in the centre with another Cumbrian great from Seaton, Tom Fletcher. He found it hard to break into the powerful Oldham team but, on Christmas Day 1901, he played in the forwards for the first time in an 11-0 home derby victory over Rochdale Hornets and became a regular member of the pack.

His first big game, a Challenge Cup semi-final and replay against Salford in 1903, ended in disappointment with a 8-0 defeat at Broughton. In 1904/05, however, he was in the team which won the First Division Championship. Injuries and intense competition for a place in the team brought him bad luck between 1907 and 1909, when he missed a Challenge Cup final, two Championship finals, two Lancashire Cup finals and games against the Kiwis and Kangaroos.

He did, however, qualify for a Lancashire League Championship medal in 1907/08 and won another in 1909/10. By 1909 Joe was restored to favour and played in three consecutive Championship finals, all against Wigan. The first in 1909 was lost 7-3 at Salford but victories at Broughton in 1910 (13-7) and 1911 (20-7) were more than adequate recompense.

His ill luck returned in the 1911/12 season. His last game of the season was the Lancashire Cup final on 2 December, when Oldham lost 5-12 to Rochdale Hornets at Broughton. He missed another Challenge Cup final in 1912 and his career ended in 1913.

Joe had a long and successful career for Cumberland following his debut against Cheshire in 1904. In 1907/08 Cumberland won the County Championship with Joe in the pack against Lancashire and Yorkshire. They also beat the New Zealand All Golds, when Joe and Tom Fletcher, then playing for Workington, were paired in the centres and took good care of the legendary Dally Messenger. He continued to bolster the Cumberland pack until 1911, but was drafted on to the wing for his last county game, a 5-2 defeat to the Australians at Maryport.

Geoff Palmer

Left centre

First-class debut
20 August 1955, Halifax v. Warrington (home)
Last game
26 April 1961, Halifax v. Oldham (home)
Cumberland debut
19 September 1955,
v. Lancashire at Workington
Cumberland caps
5, 1955-58
Club
Halifax

A native of Maryport, Geoff Palmer signed for Halifax on 21 May 1955 from Rosslyn Park RU club. The season just ended had seen him appear four times in the County Championship for Middlesex, while he had also made an appearance for Newport in 1953 when serving in the Royal Artillery. He did, however, also have experience of Rugby League, having played for Glasson Rangers in the Cumberland League.

He was an immediate success at Halifax. Geoff Palmer was a mountainous man, almost 6ft 2in and more than 15st. He was fast, too, which made him a formidable opponent for outside backs, and on his best days he made the game look ridiculously easy.

He quickly won a place in Cumberland's XIII, making his debut in an 20-18 defeat by Lancashire at Derwent Park, having played a mere seven first-team games. The three-quarter line of Southward, Gibson, Palmer and Lewthwaite was probably as good as any Cumberland ever fielded. Geoff's career for the county was short, however, and ended disastrously when he was in the team hammered 60-12 in a record defeat by Lancashire at Wigan in 1958.

Geoff played in his first final in only his thir-

teenth appearance for Halifax, a torrid Yorkshire Cup final against Hull at Headingley on 22 October 1955, which ended in a 10-10 draw. The replay brought him a winner's medal as Halifax won 7-0. His first season also took him to Wembley and to the Championship final. Palmer did as much as anyone to get Halifax to the Empire Stadium, scoring twice at Widnes in the first round, getting another against Workington in the second and claiming a match-winning brace in the semi-final at Odsal when Wigan were beaten 11-10. Wembley proved a disappointment, however, as 'Fax were beaten 13-2 by St Helens. A week later Geoff scored a super try against Hull at Maine Road, only to see Hull snatch the Championship with a last gasp 10-9 victory.

The 1957/58 season was a good one for him. He became Halifax captain and led them to the Yorkshire League Championship. He also came close to selection for the 1958 Lions tour, captaining the Greens against the Whites in a tour trial at Swinton, which had to be abandoned because of snow.

Geoff played at Thrum Hall alongside two excellent centres in Tommy Lynch, the former All Black, and Yorkshire county cap, John Burnett. It was, however, his partnership with flying Welsh winger Johnny Freeman which really captured the fans' admiration. The pair were simply breathtaking and tries oozed out of them. Freeman broke the club record with 48 tries in 1956/57 and Palmer himself ran over for 27.

Geoff Palmer's career was all too short. He retired in 1961, aged twenty-six. He had scored 102 tries for Halifax in 208 games.

Kevin Pape
Centre

First-class debut
2 September 1984, Carlisle v. Doncaster (home)
Last game
8 December 1995,
Workington Town v. Sheffield Eagles (away)
Cumbria debut
15 October 1985,
v. New Zealanders at Whitehaven
Cumbria caps
6, 1985-94
Clubs
Carlisle, Workington Town

'They say he could catch pigeons', is an expression often used about exceptionally quick sportsmen. Well, Kevin Pape could – in two ways. Outside of Rugby League his passion was pigeon racing, while as a player he was an absolute flier himself.

Not many Rugby League players score over 200 tries in a career and for any player to perform such a feat without leaving Cumbria to play for one of the big teams is more or less unheard of, particularly in modern times.

Kevin Pape played stand-off as an amateur for Glasson Rangers and signed for the three-year-old Carlisle club on 29 July 1984. He remained there for ten years, turning down offers to join more successful clubs. In the process he set records which, with the demise of the club in 1997, will never be broken.

Carlisle did not bother playing Kevin in the reserves. He went straight into the first team, scored tries in his first three games and did not miss a game until 14 September 1986, a run of 73 consecutive appearances. He picked a good match to miss, for St Helens butchered Carlisle 112-0 in a Lancashire Cup-tie.

Kevin played only eighteen games at stand-off for Carlisle and a couple on the wing. The rest were played at centre, where his eye for an opening and the pace to get through it stupified many a defence. Many of his tries were thrilling long distance affairs and his instinct for try-scoring was reminiscent of such poachers as Garry Schofield and Greg Austin. He could defend aggressively too but rarely suffered injury. Amazingly, he completed four seasons as an ever-present at

Carlisle, a very rare achievement.

Tries came in bucketfuls – he reached double figures in nine of his ten full seasons. His best season was 1993/94 when he scored 24 for Carlisle, one short of the club record. In 1987 in a Challenge Cup replay against Rochdale Hornets he equalled the club record of four in a match. By the time he had finished at Carlisle he held the club records for appearances (324), tries (192) and points (768), the latter being overtaken by Willie Richardson.

Kevin left Carlisle for Workington Town in 1994, making his debut at St Helens on 11 December in a 10-48 defeat. He went on to score fifteen tries in 36 appearances for Town and for the only time in his career played First Division rugby.

By the time Kevin played the game Cumberland had become Cumbria and there was no longer a County Championship. He did, however, win six caps for Cumbria without playing against another county! His appearances were against touring sides – versus the Australians (3), New Zealand, Papua New Guinea and France. In his last game in 1994 against the Kangaroos he captained the county and there has not been another fixture since then.

Jimmy Parkinson

Full-back, centre, wing

First-class debut
5 September 1908,
Hunslet v. Ebbw Vale (home)
Last game
22 April 1922, Oldham v. Huddersfield
(home), Championship semi-final
Cumberland debut
3 October 1908, v. Lancashire at Workington
Cumberland caps
9, 1908-22
Clubs
Hunslet, Coventry, Oldham

Jimmy Parkinson was born in Barrow in 1889 but moved in infancy to Workington. His father, Tom, played rugby for Workington and was capped as a winger by Cumberland at both Rugby Union and Northern Union. Tom had several Workington pubs, including the Grapes Hotel, the Black Lion and the Moss Bay Hotel.

By fifteen Jimmy was in the senior Workington team, when it won the Cumberland Cup and the Cumberland League. Hunslet, the pre-eminent club in the game, signed him in 1908.

Jimmy's talents – he was quick, intelligent and a fearless tackler – were recognised immediately by the county selectors. After only three games with Hunslet he played on the wing against Lancashire at Workington. It was a meteoric rise but ended catastrophically. He collided heavily with his opposing winger, Jim Leytham, and broke his collar-bone, which put him out of the game until February 1909.

Remarkably his next senior appearance was in another county game – against the Australians at Carlisle on 4 February 1909. It was a brute of a match, played in a morass and with much bad feeling. Towards the end James Lomas, the Cumberland captain, kicked through from his own line and, together with Jimmy, began a dribble which ended in Jimmy scoring 100 yards down-field to crown a historic 11-2 victory.

In 1910 Jimmy joined the newly formed Coventry club, spent three years there, establishing himself as one of the game's best full-backs and became club captain. When Coventry folded in 1913 Jimmy returned north to Oldham. Within a year he had joined up with the Oldham Territorials. He soon transferred to the Manchester Regiment, eventually rising to the rank of lieutenant, and was decorated for gallantry. While training recruits to throw grenades from a deep trench, one grenade, on a five-second fuse, failed to clear the trench. Jimmy saved at least three lives by grabbing the grenade and throwing it into the air before it exploded. He was less lucky in 1918 in France when a bullet went through his left breast.

Shortly after he had been invalided home, Jimmy played two games in one afternoon. After playing for an Army side in a curtain-raiser to the Hull-Hunslet fixture, he turned out for Hunslet in the main event.

Returning to Oldham, he played in two Lancashire Cup finals in 1919. The first at Salford on 10 May marked the return of competitive peacetime rugby but Oldham lost 22-0 to Rochdale Hornets. Jimmy played on the wing that afternoon but was full-back when the two teams met again at Salford in the final on 6 December, earning a winner's medal as Oldham triumphed 7-0.

Jimmy ultimately he became president of Oldham and died a month short of his 100th birthday in March 1989.

First-class debut
3 April 1965,
Workington Town v. Liverpool City (home)
Last game
24 April 1977, Swinton v. York (home)
Cumberland debut
12 October 1966, v. Lancashire at
Warrington
Cumberland caps
6, 1966-69
Clubs
Workington Town, Swinton, Bradford
Northern

Having played amateur Rugby League with Risehow, Bill Pattinson began his professional career at Workington Town with a substitute appearance in a 48-2 drubbing of Liverpool City in 1965. In four years with Town he developed into a high class loose-forward, big, keen, hard-running and fast. He could score tries too, as 31 in 112 appearances for Town testify. He also kicked a couple of goals.

In 1969 he moved from Workington to Warrington for a big fee but played only one season there (25 appearances, four tries). He did, however, have the good fortune to have picked the season that the Australian 'immortal' Bobbie Fulton graced Wilderspool.

Bill transferred to Swinton, scoring twice on his debut, a 24-7 home victory over Hull on 22 August 1970. Swinton were still a power and contested the Lancashire Cup final in 1972 but lost 11-25 in the final to Salford at Warrington. Bill had Cumbrian pack-mates that afternoon in Bill Holliday and Rod Smith. After 68 games (12 tries, 3 goals) Bill moved on to Bradford Northern. His first game for them, on 28 January 1973, was in a 17-4 win over Whitehaven at Odsal in a Challenge Cup first round tie.

Northern then surprised everyone by dumping Hull KR, Wigan and Dewsbury out of the Cup and getting to Wembley, despite finishing 23rd in the league. Bill was now usually operating as a second-rower. Featherstone Rovers ended the fairy-tale by hammering Bradford 33-14 in the final and Bill received his second runners-up medal in a season.

In 1973/74 he received a winner's medal as Northern won the Second Division Championship and there was another winner's award in 1974/75, when Northern beat Widnes 3-2 in the John Player Trophy final at a mud-bound Wilderspool, Bill being on the substitute's bench for the game. He played 64 games (7 tries, 1 goal) for Bradford and returned for a final spell at Swinton in 1975, making his second debut for them on 17 August in an 8-10 defeat by St Helens at Station Road. Unfortunately, the Lions suffered relegation in 1975/76 and Bill played his last season in the Second Division.

Bill won an England Under 24s cap on 26 November 1966 in a surprising 7-4 defeat by France at Bayonne. He packed down at loose-forward in a very strong-looking side – his second-rowers were Bob Haigh and Bob Irving – but the dismissal of two Englishmen and a French player marred the proceedings.

His Cumberland career began six weeks previously when Cumberland, fielding ten Workington players, won the County Championship with a tremendous 18-14 win against Lancashire at Warrington. Bill bagged two of the winners' tries. The other highlight of his county career was Cumberland's 17-15 triumph over the 1967 Australians at Workington, when Bill's opposing loose-forward was Kangaroo legend Johnny Raper.

First-class debut
5 October 1975,
Workington Town v. Rochdale Hornets (away)
Last game
29 March 1987,
Workington Town v. Mansfield (away)
Cumbria debut
8 October 1980,
v. New Zealanders at Whitehaven
Cumbria caps
6, 1980-86
England caps
2
Club
Workington Town

As an amateur Billy Pattinson was hot property. He played for Broughton Moor, Cockermouth and Cumberland and he was capped by Great Britain in the first BARLA international match ever played, when France were beaten 10-4 in Lyon on 9 March 1975.

He chose to join his local professional club, Workington Town, and remained loyal to them for the whole of his career. Billy was a gangling loose-forward, who stood 6ft 2in and weighed 14st, although he never looked that heavy. He was a heck of a forward, very quick and long-striding, with a debilitating side-step, a devastating line in cover tackling, the ability to go the full eighty minutes, an aggressive streak which he learned to temper and a grin like a Cheshire cat. His reluctance to leave Workington probably cost him a bagful of medals and caps.

Billy's debut in 1975 came in a rarity – a try-less Rugby League match – when Town drew 2-2 at Rochdale Hornets. Billy scored two tries in a 25-14 home loss to Leigh on 1 February 1976. They were the first of 67 he would amass for the club over twelve seasons. Town were promoted to Division One at the end of Billy's first season.

His first four years with Workington were that mini golden age when Town contested four consecutive Lancashire Cup finals and the club could still harbour ambitions of returning to the very top flight. Billy played in all four, the first three at loose-forward and the last in the second-row. Naturally, the most memorable was 1977 when Town thrillingly beat Wigan 16-13 at Warrington. The other three, however, all provided Billy with runners-up medals, as each time Widnes proved too good, all the games being at Central Park, Wigan.

From 1980/81, however, when Town were relegated, things were never the same. Five seasons running the team yo-yoed between the divisions, winning promotion in 1981/82 and 1983/84, only to go down again each time. Billy was a constant eloquent reminder of what a class player could do in the right circumstances. He had chances to leave – Hull apparently offered £55,000 to Town – but Billy toughed it out until he retired in 1987, having put in 321 action-packed appearances.

In the circumstances Billy must have been special, for England did cap him twice. His debut on 21 February 1981, as a half-time substitute for Brian Case, was an anti-climax. In a truly dreadful match at Headingley, England lost 5-1, referee Guy Cattaneo's performance beggaring description. Billy played in England's next match at second-row on 18 March, enjoying a 17-4 victory over Wales at Craven Park, Hull.

Billy had to wait until 1980 for his Cumbria debut, starring in a 9-3 win against the Kiwis at Whitehaven. In 1985 he played against them again, less happily, being sent off in a 32-6 defeat.

Albert Pepperell
Scrum-half

First-class debut
5 September 1942,
Huddersfield v. Keighley (away)
Last game
2 October 1954,
Workington Town v. Wigan (home)
Cumberland debut
26 January 1946, v. Lancashire at Workington
Cumberland caps
12, 1946-54
Test caps
2
Clubs
Huddersfield, Workington Town

Albert Pepperell was born in Siddick in 1922 and, like his father, Simeon, and brothers, Stanley and Russ, he played his amateur rugby for Seaton. It seemed natural that he should follow his brothers to Huddersfield when he turned professional in 1942. Unlike his more versatile brothers, Albert was a specialist scrum-half. There were few first-team chances for Albert but on Christmas Day 1942 all three brothers played together for the first time in the Huddersfield team which defeated Halifax 5-4 at Fartown.

Albert's career at Fartown saw him make 29 appearances (four tries). Included amongst them was the two-legged Challenge Cup final of 1945 when Huddersfield defeated Bradford Northern 13-9 on aggregate.

When peacetime football returned, Workington Town had just been launched and Huddersfield agreed to sell Albert to the fledgling club. He made his Town debut at Widnes on 8 December 1945.

Albert soon won his first Cumberland cap when he appeared at stand-off in a 18-3 loss to Lancashire at Workington. The rest of his caps were won in his normal position of scrum-half, five in combination with brother Russ and one with Stan at stand-off. Cumberland had little success in the county championship in this period. There were, however, great triumphs in the 1948/49 season, when Albert played in Cumberland's 5-4 victory over the Australians at Whitehaven and both Yorkshire and Lancashire were overcome to lift a rare championship. Albert

had also scored a vital try in Town's historic 10-7 win over the Kangaroos.

Albert had developed into a top-notch scrum-half with Town. He was crafty, cool-headed, able to vary his tactics, sound in defence and capable of finding chinks in tight defences. Physically, at 5ft 7in and over 11st, he was quite sturdy for his position. Despite two severe jaw injuries in 1949/50, Albert was one of the surprise selections to tour Australasia. Albert, the first ever Cumbrian scrum-half to tour, had a good trip, scoring seven tries in eleven games and appearing in the first test against New Zealand at Christchurch.

He won another test cap against the Kiwis in the third test of 1951 at Headingley, which Britain won 16-12, and played for a British Empire XIII which defeated the New Zealanders 26-2 at Chelsea on 23 January 1952.

Albert was one third of a wonderful scrum-base trio with Billy Ivison and Jackie Thomas in Workington's greatest triumphs – the 1951 Championship final victory over Warrington and the Wembley defeat of Featherstone in 1952. His career was ended when he was thirty-two by a dreadful ankle injury. Albert Pepperell deserved a much better finale. He had played 240 games for Workington, scoring 57 tries and 5 goals.

Russ Pepperell

Utility back

First-class debut
30 September 1939,
Huddersfield v. Keighley (home)
Last game
21 April 1956, Huddersfield v. Keighley (away)
Cumberland debut
4 January 1947, v. Lancashire at Barrow
Cumberland caps
16, 1947-54
England caps
4
Club
Huddersfield

Of the three Pepperell brothers Russ was the most versatile, excelling in any of the back positions. In his last season as an amateur with Seaton, 1938/39, he played for Cumberland against Lancashire and Yorkshire. He was so outstanding that he was chosen to captain England Amateurs against France at Bordeaux.

Russ signed for Huddersfield, for whom Stan Pepperell already played, on 3 December 1938. By the time Russ was drafted into the first team at Huddersfield the Second World War had broken out. Service in the Royal Artillery reduced his opportunities with Huddersfield but enabled him to play representative rugby, league and union, for Northern Command.

On 23 January 1943 at Headingley, Russ appeared at full-back in one of the landmark matches in the history of rugby, when a Rugby League XV met a Rugby Union XV for the first time, under RU laws. The Rugby League XV triumphed 18-11. Russ was the solitary Cumbrian in the RL side.

At 5ft 7in and around 11st (rising to 12st 11lb by the end of his career), Russ was not a big man but he was intelligent, elusive and brave. Moreover, he was renowned for his sportsmanship and leadership. His first county game, in January 1947, was in a scoreless draw against Lancashire at Barrow, when he played centre. His next game, against Yorkshire at Leeds, saw

him at full-back and elevated to the captaincy. He won 16 Cumberland caps, most of them at stand-off and more often than not he skippered the team.

Russ' ability to play any back position was a huge benefit to Huddersfield but paradoxically hampered his international aspirations. He did win four England caps, including one as a winger, and was never on a losing England team. However, he never won a test cap despite being a travelling reserve on four occasions. Perhaps his highest distinction was his selection as joint-captain of a glittering Empire team which toured France in May 1949.

With Huddersfield he picked up Yorkshire League Championship-winners' medals in 1948/49, 1949/50 and 1951/52 and Yorkshire Cup-winners' medals in 1950 and 1952. In the 1950 final he scored both Huddersfield's tries in a 16-3 victory over Castleford and in 1952 was captain of the Fartowners, who defeated Batley 18-8. He also played in two Championship finals, winning 13-12 against Warrington in 1949 and losing 20-2 against Wigan in 1950.

Russ completed a full set of major honours in 1953, when, as captain-coach, he led his team to Wembley. Huddersfield were underdogs to St Helens but triumphed 15-10 as Saints resorted to some very questionable tactics. He became only the third – and last – Cumbrian captain to have led a team to victory in the Challenge Cup final.

Retiring in 1956, Russ Pepperell briefly coached Keighley but then emigrated to Australia, where he coached Manly-Warringah in 1964 and 1965.

Stanley Pepperell
Stand-off, scrum-half

First-class debut
15 December 1934,
Huddersfield v. Dewsbury (home)
Last game
22 October 1949,
Huddersfield v. Bramley (home)
Cumberland debut
10 October 1936, v. Yorkshire at Workington
Cumberland caps
11, 1936-49
England caps
3
Club
Huddersfield

Stan Pepperell was the oldest of the three multi-talented Pepperell brothers and was born in Seaton in 1914. When he was twenty he won selection at stand-off for Cumberland amateurs, who beat Lancashire and Yorkshire in October 1934 to win the County Championship. He was subsequently snapped up by Huddersfield, for whom he made his first-team debut against Dewsbury a couple of months later.

As a stand-off he was an adept provider for other players, an ideal link-man. He was particularly quick to see openings and a master of the grubber kick. Although only around 5ft 6in tall and 11st 7lb, he was a solid and courageous tackler. There were always arguments as to whether he was a better stand-off than scrum-half but wherever he played, the team benefitted. Besides, full-back, centre and wing were not beyond his domain and he could kick goals.

His most prolific season for goals was 1935/36, when he landed 43 for Huddersfield, but in the following season his points tally was 141 from 23 tries and 36 goals. That 1936/37 season saw Stan in such good form that he won both county and international recognition. On 10 October he partnered Billy Little at half-back as Cumberland defeated Yorkshire 16-10 at Workington, to commence a county career which would span thirteen years. Cumberland made the most of his versatility by employing him at full-back, centre, stand-off and scrum-half. On 7 January 1947, in a scoreless draw against Lancashire at Barrow, he captained the Cumberland team which contained both his brothers.

At international level he made his England debut less than a month after he had played his first county game. He was drafted in on the wing at the last minute, when Salford's Barney Hudson withdrew from the game against Wales at Pontypridd on 7 November 1936. England lost 2-3. Stan did enough to retain his place, but at stand-off, as England beat France 23-9 at Halifax on 10 April 1937. A third and final England cap came his way in 1944 when he dropped two goals in a 9-9 draw with Wales at Wigan. In 1938 he had toured France with a Rugby League squad.

At domestic level, Stan was not too lucky. He played in three Yorkshire Cup finals, in 1937, 1938 and 1942, but was only a winner in the second when Hull were beaten 18-10 in the first major final to be staged at Odsal Stadium. Huddersfield lost to Castleford at Wembley in his first season at Fartown, but Stan was still understudying regular half-backs Gwyn Richards and Dai Davies. In 1945 Huddersfield won the Cup in a two-leg final against Bradford but Stan's RAF commitments meant he was unavailable.

His Fartown career yielded Stan 280 appearances in which he amassed 508 points. There would have been many more but for the war.

First-class debut
4 March 1961, Oldham v. Salford (away)
Last game
20 April 1968, Bradford Northern v. Wigan (home) Top Sixteen Play-off
Cumberland debut
16 September 1964, v. Lancashire at Blackpool
Cumberland caps
4, 1964-67
Test caps
1
Clubs
Oldham, Bradford Northern

Johnny Rae was a product of the Wath Brow ARL club but spent his entire professional career in Lancashire and Yorkshire. Although he achieved county and test status, his career was riddled with injury, depriving him of the opportunity to achieve even more. His playing came to a halt when he was only twenty-seven because of a severe knee injury.

His first club was Oldham, who had a long history of importing Cumbrians. In his time at Watersheddings he played in a pack containing former Whitehaven star Geoff Robinson and prop Alf Mumberson from Aspatria. Johnny was 6ft 2in tall, lean and fast. His natural position appeared to be loose-forward but Oldham employed him predominantly in the second-row. He was versatile enough, however, for Oldham to use him once on the wing and once at hooker!

In three and a half years at Oldham Johnny played only 41 first-team games, scoring a dozen tries. The biggest game in which he appeared was a Lancashire Cup semi-final in 1962, when St Helens sneaked a 10-8 victory at Watersheddings. His last game for Oldham was a 35-8 home victory over Barrow on 21 September 1963.

A transfer to the newly reformed Bradford Northern for £1,250 signalled a much more successful period for Johnny. He made his debut in the revived Northern's opening fixture on 22 August 1964, when Hull KR beat them 34-20 at Odsal. Terry Ackerley, a

fellow Cumbrian and brother of test player Alvin, was also in the pack as hooker. Northern used Johnny almost exclusively at loose-forward and his drive, enthusiasm, covering and penchant for try-scoring were revelatory as he and the team exceeded all expectations.

Three weeks after his Odsal debut Johnny made his first appearance for Cumberland, figuring in the second-row with Bill Holliday, in a 13-11 victory over Lancashire at Blackpool. The following season, 1965/66, he earned a County Championship winner's medal, playing on the left wing in a 19-3 win against Yorkshire at Craven Park, Hull, and scoring a try from loose-forward in a 14-11 defeat of Lancashire at Whitehaven.

That 1965/66 season was certainly Johnny's most memorable. In the opening game of the Kiwi tour he was a try-scorer in Bradford's 28-15 victory. Northern's form was so good that they reached the Yorkshire Cup final on 16 October, upsetting all calculations when they beat Hunslet 17-8 at Headingley. A week later Johnny was capped by Great Britain on his home ground at Odsal, when New Zealand were beaten 15-9. Three other Cumbrians, Paul Charlton, Bill Holliday and Brian Edgar were in the team, whose skipper was Northern's scrum-half Tommy Smales. Johnny, Smales and stand-off Dave Stockwell were the fulcrum for Northern's successful revival.

Johnny's last season brought him a final Cumberland cap and an appearance against the Kangaroos for Northern. In 132 games for the club he scored 40 tries and 9 goals.

John Risman

Utility back, loose-forward

First-class debut
6 April 1971,
Workington Town v. Huyton (away)
Last game
2 May 1984, Carlisle v. Hunslet (home)
Cumbria debut
12 September 1973, v. Yorkshire at Bramley
Cumbria caps
14, 1973-79
Wales caps
3
Clubs
Workington Town, Blackpool Borough,
Fulham, Carlisle

Of course, everyone knows that John Risman had a great Rugby League pedigree. He was the son of Gus, the Hall of Famer, Lions captain and the catalyst for the success of Workington Town in their greatest days. His older brother Bev was a Great Britain captain and a Rugby Union Lion. Gus was a genius and Bev a great.

John therefore had a lot to live up to when he left the Carlisle RU club to join Workington Town in 1971. He achieved much in his own right in a long career, which lasted thirteen years and took in over 300 games. He inherited some of the Risman genes in that he was very versatile, full-back, wing and centre all being his province, while in his latter days he switched successfully to loose-forward.

The bulk of his career was played at Derwent Park, where his 6ft, twelve and a half stone frame, flitted about Workington's back-line, wherever and whenever it was needed. In 212 full appearances (he also made ten as substitute) for Town, 45 were at full-back, 85 on the wing and 82 at centre. Tom Mitchell described him as 'strong and daunting' and he was renowned for his reliability and tackling prowess.

Like most of the players from that era at Workington, his career highlight was the winning of the Lancashire Cup against Wigan in 1977, when he played right centre. He was also in the team which lost to Widnes in the 1978 final. He had missed the final of 1976 against Widnes, having played in the first two rounds.

On leaving Town in 1980 he moved briefly to Blackpool Borough, scoring his only try of the season in one of the all-time great shock results when Borough won 18-15 at Leeds. For the 1980/81 season, he went south to London and helped Fulham to gain promotion in their first season in Rugby League. For 1981/82 he returned to Blackpool but left in February 1982 for Carlisle, helping them to promotion. He ended his career there in 1984.

At representative level John won county and international honours. He made his debut for Cumbria against Yorkshire in 1973 and went on to win fourteen caps, including appearances against the Australians in 1973 at Whitehaven and 1978 at Barrow. He played in all four three-quarter positions for Cumbria.

John followed in his father's massive footsteps by playing for Wales. He made his international debut at full-back on 15 January 1978 in a 29-7 win against France at Widnes. On 4 February 1979, he was a late substitute in Narbonne when the French gained revenge, winning 15-8. His third cap, on 16 March 1979, saw him at right centre as partner to Clive Sullivan but England beat Wales 15-7 at Widnes.

First-class debut
7 September 1901, Hull v. Runcorn (home)
Last game
6 October 1906,
Cumberland v. Lancashire at Maryport
Cumberland debut
13 April 1904, v. Cheshire at Birkenhead
Cumberland caps
4, 1904-06
Yorkshire caps
1, 1902
Durham & Northumberland caps
7, 1902-03
Club
Hull

Jim Ritson had an extraordinary, and probably unique, career in county rugby, playing at that level for three counties at Rugby League and for two at Rugby Union – and all within six years.

He was born in Cockermouth in 1879 and was playing in Cockermouth RU's first XV by the time he was eighteen. In his first county match in 1898/99 he scored three tries against Westmorland. He then began his travels, playing union for Wallsend, Walker, Rockcliffe and South Shields. He thus qualified to play for Northumberland in 1900/01, one of the games of his life being against Lancashire at Liverpool when he scored twice. He also came close to an England cap, figuring in the North v. South trials and being selected as reserve for three internationals.

In 1901 Jim turned professional with Hull and was soon captain of the team. He was a forward of great mobility. Physically he was not big – 5ft 9in and 12st 4lb – but he was a human dynamo, often popping up in the back movements and forever cover-tackling. He played for his various counties at wing, centre, half-back and forward. In 1903 he was described thus, 'Ritson is a typical Cumbrian, broad-shouldered, and the perfection of muscular development. There is nothing extraordinary about his appearance, but he

would be a keen critic who would find fault with this well-proportioned individual'.

Jim's career at Hull lasted four years in which he made 84 appearances and scored 16 tries, his last game being a 13-7 victory at Brighouse Rangers on 16 December 1905. Hull were a middle of the table side in his time at The Boulevard, the nearest he came to trophy success with them being an appearance in the Challenge Cup semi-final against Halifax in 1903.

Residence in Hull allowed him to play for Yorkshire. He only won one cap, however, appearing in a Roses match at The Boulevard on 15 February 1902 in a 13-8 victory. The following season he decided to play for Durham & Northumberland, newcomers to the County Championship. Ironically, he made his debut against Cumberland at Workington in a 0-5 loss. He went on to play seven times for the twin counties before the game there died. Two of those games, both at South Shields in 1903, saw Jim on victorious sides – against Cheshire and his native county.

On 13 April 1904, he made his debut for Cumberland in a 2-5 defeat by Cheshire at Birkenhead. By 1905 he had begun to play for Egremont, although Hull held his registration until 1909. In 1905/06 Cumberland and Lancashire tied for the Championship and a 3-3 draw at Wigan in a play-off failed to settle the issue. Jim Ritson must have been tired after it – there were 134 scrums!

Geoff Robinson
Second-row, loose-forward, prop

First-class debut
14 August 1954,
Whitehaven v. Belle Vue Rangers (home)
Last game
9 January 1965, Oldham v. Barrow (away)
Cumberland debut
6 September 1956, v. Lancashire at Wigan
Cumberland caps
5, 1956-62
Clubs
Whitehaven, Oldham

In 1954 Whitehaven beat off considerable opposition to sign the Workington and Cumberland Rugby Union back-rower Geoff Robinson. Whatever the cost, it was money well spent. He went straight into the first team and was progressing well when he broke his arm, just after scoring his first try at Oldham, on 20 November 1954.

At 6ft 2in, he was tall for a Rugby League forward but he had good handling skills, a long stride and the ability to break tackles. He was an eye-catcher, who was at times brilliant. Returning from injury he formed a formidable second-row with Steve McCourt during 1955/56. However, with the emergence of Dick Huddart he moved to loose-forward for the 1956/57 season, when he scored a dozen tries and starred in the famous run to the Cup semi-finals. In his last season at Whitehaven he bagged 11 tries in 22 games, including three against York on 16 August 1958. He scored his 36th try in his 139th and last game for 'Haven, a 47-2 defeat of Rochdale on 2 May 1959.

Geoff played just five games for Cumberland, two of which were won. In those games he played loose-forward, second-row and prop. He wrote his name in the history books on 16 September 1957, when he became the first forward to score a hat-trick for Cumberland as they beat Lancashire 22-12 at Workington. He would not play for Cumberland for another five years.

In 1959 Geoff was transferred to Oldham, for whom he would play 177 games (20 tries). The £9,000 fee was the biggest yet for a forward. He joined another Cumbrian, winger Ike Southward, who a few months earlier had become the world's most expensive player

when signing from Workington. Ambitious Oldham thus had both the world's most expensive back and forward.

Unfortunately, Oldham were entering a slow decline and Geoff won no trophies at Watersheddings. In 1959/60 Oldham lost in the Challenge Cup semi-final 12-9 to Hull at Odsal – shades of Whitehaven in 1957 – and in 1962 they lost to 10-8 to St Helens in the Lancashire Cup semi-final. The 1963/64 season was the cruellest, however. Oldham lost three semi-finals – 10-0 at Leigh in the Lancashire Cup, 22-11 at St Helens in the Western Division and, most agonisingly, to Hull KR in the Challenge Cup.

A 5-5 draw at Headingley was followed by an evening replay at Swinton. Oldham drew level at 14-14 in the 79th minute to force extra time. Oldham grabbed the lead when Geoff crashed over at the corner after Rovers had spilled a high kick. He must have thought his day had come but after 92 minutes the referee abandoned the game because of poor visibility with Oldham leading 17-14 and Hull KR out on their feet. Rovers won the second replay 12-2 at Fartown.

First-class debut
14 August 1954, Workington Town v.
Featherstone Rovers (away)
Last game
27 February 1972,
Whitehaven v. Widnes (away)
Cumberland debut
30 August 1954, v. Yorkshire at Workington
Cumberland caps
21, 1954-69

John (Sol) Roper hailed from Pica, near Distington. He was a schoolboy prodigy who captained Cumberland Schools in 1951. He played for Distington and Hensingham and was selected for England Amateurs (Open Age) when he was only seventeen, scoring a try in England's 23-0 victory over France at Headingley on 17 April 1954.

A few months later Sol Roper was a first-teamer with Workington Town, striking up a decade-long telepathic understanding with Harry Archer – probably the most celebrated half-back pairing in Cumbrian history.

Sol's first season with Town, 1954/55, was eventful. Sixteen days after his Town debut he made his county debut, aged only eighteen years and two months, when he played against Yorkshire on his home ground, Borough Park.

When the Challenge Cup came round in 1955 few thought much of Town's chances but they surprised the Rugby League world. Dewsbury Celtic, Leeds and St Helens were beaten before Town accounted for Featherstone

13-2 in the semi-final at Leeds, when Sol was heavily concussed.

In the final against Barrow at Wembley, Sol was the youngest man on the pitch. Again he was in the wars. After 52 minutes he was stretchered off with a shoulder injury. Although he returned to play heroically on the wing, Barrow had established a winning lead and Town eventually lost 12-21.

In 1958 Sol was back at Wembley as Town's captain, at that time the youngest ever Wembley skipper. The final pitted them against Wigan but once again they lost (13-9), injuries being a crucial factor. It was the same story a week later in their Championship final against Hull at Odsal. This time second-rower Cec Thompson was taken from the field after 25 minutes with Town leading 3-0. He never returned and Hull won 20-3.

Sol finally picked up a winner's medal with Town in 1962, when they beat Widnes 10-0 in the inaugural Western Division Championship final at Wigan, following a 9-9 draw at the same venue. The Roper-Archer duo's superiority at half-back was a vital factor.

Sol carried on playing for Town until 1966, amassing 398 appearances. As a scrum-half he knew all the tricks of his trade. He fitted the stereotype – invariably the smallest man on the field but just as invariably the gutsiest. He was renowned for his low, clean tackling, his stamina and his guile. His total of 94 tries was testimony to his attacking values.

After a year out of the professional ranks Sol joined Whitehaven and gave five years' splendid service with 82 appearances (11 tries, 9 goals). While at the Rec he extended his Cumberland career to fifteen years, one of the longest on record.

Stan Satterthwaite
Prop-forward

First-class debut
17 March 1928, Leeds v. Castleford (home)
Last game
12 January 1946, Leeds v. Dewsbury (home)
Cumberland debut
29 September 1934, v. Yorkshire at Workington
Cumberland caps
6, 1934-45
Club
Leeds (He also guested for Batley, Huddersfield, Hunslet and Wakefield Trinity during the Second World War)

Satterthwaite is a good Cumbrian name, probably deriving from the village between Windermere and Coniston Water. As Cumbrian prop forwards went, Stan Satterthwaite was a bloody good one too. That's certainly what they would have said at Headingley, where he played for eighteen years.

Stan hailed from Workington but found fame at Leeds, for whom he first turned out in a 20-4 home win over Castleford in 1928. Getting a permanent place in the first team was no easy matter and Stan had to bide his time. It took him three years. In that time Leeds lost in three consecutive Championship finals, won the Yorkshire Cup twice and the Yorkshire League twice, and Stan had no medals at all to show. His luck turned, however, and in 1931/32 Leeds won the Challenge Cup, with Stan appearing in every round except the final but he had gained that elusive medal.

The following season he picked up a Yorkshire Cup winner's medal, although again he missed the final. 1933/34 brought him the first of three Yorkshire League Championship winners' medals, others following in 1934/35 and 1936/37. In 1934 he played in all three of Leeds' epic Yorkshire Cup final matches against Wakefield Trinity, two replays being needed before Leeds won 13-0 at Hunslet. In 1935 it was marginally easier as Leeds beat York 3-0 at Halifax to retain the trophy, Stan helping his pack to a 51-33 scrum supremacy.

One of the undoubted highlights of his career was the 1936 Challenge Cup final, when Leeds trounced Warrington 18-2 at

Wembley and Stan received his medal from Lord Derby. A pen picture of Stan remarked, 'keen, alert and a useful handler, he covers a lot of ground'. He had to that day as Warrington won the scrums 46-24. Stan went on to play in three more Challenge Cup finals – in 1941 and 1942, when Leeds beat Halifax both times at Odsal, and in 1943, when they lost 15-16 on aggregate to Dewsbury.

One of the biggest games of his life was the Championship final of 1938 at Elland Road, where Leeds lost 2-8 to local rivals Hunslet, a game which drew an English record crowd of 54,112.

Stan made his Cumberland debut in 1934 in a 10-0 victory over Yorkshire, all the points coming in the last ten minutes. Lancashire were beaten 15-5 and Stan added a County Championship winner's medal to his collection. War prevented him from earning more than six caps, the last in 1945. His only other representative honour came on 28 September 1935, when he figured in a Rugby League XIII, which beat Lyon-Villeurbanne 23-19 at York.

Stan's career at Leeds comprised 339 appearances, 25 tries and 28 goals, nineteen of which were kicked in his final season.

Bobby Scott

Full-back

First-class debut*
15 November 1922,
Cumberland v. Lancashire at Swinton
Last game
23 January 1937, Swinton v. Keighley (away)
Cumberland caps
21, 1922-35
Clubs
Batley, Huddersfield, Carlisle City, Swinton

* Scott's first class club debut was on
10 January 1925 for Batley v. Wigan (home)

Gus Risman described Bobby Scott thus, 'Safe as the Bank of England. Not spectacular but could catch a ball anywhere and from any angle. He had a knack of seemingly being able to pluck a ball away from the touch line when everyone could swear the ball was over and out of play.'

Bobby Scott was a full-back, who came from Aspatria. He was not the standard size and shape for the role, being a mere 5ft 4in and 10st 10lb. Physically he should have been a half-back but in a career stretching over 472 games he only played there twice.

Bobby began his professional career in 1925 with Batley, who were the reigning Rugby League champions. He played 103 games for Batley, scoring 8 tries and 48 goals. A couple of those goals were landed in a famous 19-17 victory over the 1926 Kiwis. His time at Batley brought no medals, however, and in 1928 he moved to Huddersfield but played only three matches there before returning to Cumberland. Bobby had joined the short-lived Carlisle City, making his debut in their opening fixture, a 10-3 home loss to Wigan Highfield. Bobby played eight games before

the club collapsed less than three months later.

His next and final stop was at Swinton, where he enjoyed considerable success over nine memorable seasons. In his first season he picked up a Lancashire League Championship medal, gaining a second in 1930/31, when he also played in Swinton's 14-7 Championship final triumph over Leeds at Wigan. In 1931/32 he collected runners-up medals for both the Lancashire Cup and the Challenge Cup. In 1933 he kicked a goal in Swinton's 5-15 defeat by Salford in his second Championship final. A third followed in 1935, when Warrington were beaten 14-3 at Wigan in his last major final.

Other highlights of his Swinton career were victories over the Australians in 1929 (9-5) and 1933 (10-4). In 337 appearances for the Lions, Bobby scored 9 tries and 124 goals.

Bobby had an outstanding career for Cumberland. His first three games for the county in 1922 and 1924 were played as a member of the Aspatria club, players from amateur clubs still being called up in emergencies. He went on to win 21 caps, 19 at full-back. This was a remarkable achievement in view of the fact that he was a contemporary of Jim Brough and Joe Oliver, who were both world class full-backs and internationals. The selectors chose, however, to play the diminutive Bobby Scott at the back and pushed Brough and Oliver into the centres. Bobby earned County Championship medals in 1927/28, 1933/34 and 1934/35. Undoubtedly the greatest performance of the county in his time was the last minute 17-16 defeat of the Australians at Whitehaven in 1933.

Bill Smith
Winger, centre

First-class debut
25 December 1950,
Whitehaven v. Liverpool Stanley (home)
Last game
28 April 1962,
Whitehaven v. Blackpool Borough (home)
Cumberland debut
15 September 1954, v. Lancashire at Wigan
Cumberland caps
5, 1954-57
Club
Whitehaven

Bill Smith's Whitehaven career record of 148 tries stood for 40 years before David Seeds surpassed the figure in 2002. That fact is a measure of just how much Bill stood above generations of wingers who succeeded him at the Recreation Ground. Yet for his first four years with Whitehaven Bill played at centre and did not look a likely record-breaker.

He had begun his Rugby League career as an amateur with Kells and made his debut for Whitehaven on Christmas Day 1950. His first try was scored in an 8-8 home draw with Wigan on 13 December 1952 but he did not start to produce large numbers of touchdowns until he moved permanently out to the wing half-way through the 1954/55 season, claiming his first hat-trick in a 14-9 win at Liverpool City on 2 April 1955.

Bill was a handful as a winger, nearly 6ft tall and over 13st. He was strong and direct and was reputedly an even-timer for the 100 yards. He had a nice line in cover defence too.

The 1956/57 season was a big one for Bill and the club. Whitehaven came within a few minutes of reaching Wembley, going out 10-9 in the semis to Leeds at Odsal. Oddly enough, Bill did not score in any of that year's Cup-ties, but he did score a classic try in conjunction with Billy Banks and Syd Lowdon against the Australians on 20 October, when Whitehaven beat the tourists 14-11. That was just one of 29 he scored in the season to create a new club record.

The following season he bagged another 23 tries, including a four-match sequence in which he crossed for twelve – three at Bradford Northern, four at home to Rochdale Hornets,

two at St Helens and another three at the Rec against Blackpool.

In 1958/59 he just failed to beat his own record in scoring 28 tries but he did set a personal best by claiming four in a first round Challenge Cup-tie against Liverpool City. He also became the first Whitehaven player to amass 100 tries, when he crossed in a famous 24-12 victory over Wigan on 25 August 1958.

The tries did slow down after 1959, but Bill still produced some outstanding performances over the next three years. One of the best was a hat-trick in a 23-14 triumph against Hull at The Boulevard on 25 March 1961, a ground where few visiting wingers found much joy. He finished his career in style by scoring twice against Blackpool in his final appearance at the Rec.

Bill's career with Cumberland was strangely sparse, five caps and a solitary try being the consequence of playing at a time when Jim Lewthwaite, Ivor Watts, Ike Southward and Syd Lowdon provided plenty of competition for the wing spots.

Fergie Southward

Centre, winger

First-class debut
22 January 1921, Salford v. Barrow (home)
Last game
8 April 1933, Salford v. St Helens Recs (home)
Cumberland debut
28 October 1922, v. Yorkshire at Maryport
Cumberland caps
26, 1922-32
Club
Salford

Ferguson Southward was the outstanding Salford player of the 1920s, which was a period of depression for the club. Fergie was a ray of sunlight in a team which finished bottom of the league in his first season, 1920/21 at The Willows and not much higher until 1928, when success suddenly embraced the club. It is fair to say that from 1921 to 1928 Fergie did the bulk of the team's scoring in terms of both tries and goals. He was almost a one man band.

Fergie was a native of Dearham and played his amateur rugby for Dearham and Brookland Rovers along with his brother Isaac, who was the father of the great winger of the 1950s and 1960s, Ike Southward. Fergie was equally adept at wing and centre, his pace and elusiveness disconcerting many a defence, while he could also turn his skills to half-back, when required. He was a fine goal-kicker too.

His career with Salford encompassed 340 appearances in which he claimed 586 points from 90 tries and 158 goals. He scored his first

try in a 21-6 home victory over newcomers to the league Featherstone Rovers on 5 November 1921, and a week later kicked his first two goals at St Helens Recs, where Salford lost 10-15.

On 22 September 1923 Fergie partnered Jim Lomas, who was making a brief comeback, in the Salford centre with a 19-6 victory against Widnes at The Willows. A few years later he partnered Gus Risman regularly in the centres. He was the only man to partner those two icons.

Things appeared to be looking up in 1926/27 as Salford reached the semi-finals of the Lancashire Cup, in which they held St Helens Recs to a replay but lost 14-0 at home. The New Zealanders were given a scare before Salford went down 18-10 with Fergie landing two goals. At least he had the satisfaction of scoring his only hat-trick in a 20-7 home success against Pontypridd.

Salford finally turned the corner in 1928/29 reaching the Championship semi-final, repeating the achievement in 1929/30, when they also lost in the Lancashire Cup final. Fergie missed the final, but in 1931 he won the Lancashire Cup for his team with the last kick of the game as Salford beat Swinton 10-8 in the final at Broughton. His last season brought him deserved winners' medals for the Lancashire League and for the Championship, although he did not play in the final.

Fergie's record with Cumberland was tremendous. He won a massive 26 caps, played wing, centre, stand-off and scrum-half and became captain in 1931. He was in the team which took the County Championship in 1927/28 and fittingly crowned his career by captaining the team to another Championship in 1932/33, his final season in the game.

Ike Southward
Right winger

First-class debut
23 August 1952,
Workington Town *v.* Warrington (away)
Last game
1 February 1969,
Whitehaven *v.* Warrington (home)
Cumberland debut
30 August 1954, *v.* Yorkshire at Workington
Cumberland caps
12, 1954-67
Test caps
11
Clubs
Workington Town, Oldham, Whitehaven

Along with Tom Mitchell and Gus Risman, there is little doubt that Ike Southward is one of the three most significant figures in the history of Workington Town. Certainly no one has given more to Town than Ike in such a variety of capacities from player to coach, from groundsman to director and most things in between.

It is as a truly great wingman that he will best be remembered, however. Fast, direct and determined, Ike was an absolute terror to defences throughout the Rugby League playing world. In a seventeen-year career which took in a couple of years with Oldham and a few months with Whitehaven, Ike Southward set and broke records, won the highest honours for his country and established a reputation as monumental as any Cumbrian who has played the game.

Born on 15 August 1934, Ike made his name playing amateur Rugby League for Glasson Rangers before signing for Workington Town. His first-team debut as an eighteen-year-old stand-off was inauspicious as Town went down 26-2 at Warrington on 23 August 1952. Thereafter, however, it was almost all good news. Within two years he had made the first of the dozen appearances he would make for Cumberland in a county career which stretched over thirteen years. Oddly, his first and last games for the county were played as a centre, the rest in his normal position on the wing. His county debut ended in a 27-0 mauling by Yorkshire, while his last game for Cumberland, on his home ground at Derwent Park, saw a famous 17-15 victory over the Australians on 18 November 1967.

At club level Ike was sensational from the start. In his second full season (1954/55) he bagged 33 tries for Town and won a Challenge Cup runners-up medal as Workington lost 21-12 to Barrow at Wembley.

On 17 September 1955 against Blackpool Borough, Ike scored an amazing 33 points from seven tries and six goals. Those seven tries remain a Town record almost half a century later. Perhaps an even more amazing feat, however, occurred on 31 January 1959, when he outshone the immortal Brian Bevan in running in five tries as Town beat Warrington, an infinitely tougher nut than Blackpool, 32-15. In 1958 Town reached both the Challenge Cup final and the Championship final but lost 13-9 to Wigan at Wembley and 3-20 to Hull at Odsal. Ike scored all Town's points in the two games. Agonisingly he lost the ball in the act of scoring late in the game at Wembley, when a try and a conversion would almost certainly have brought the Cup back to Cumberland.

By 1959 Ike was established as one of the game's great attractions. As a winger he was bracketed alongside Billy Boston and Mick Sullivan as the best of British in that position. He was so outstanding that Oldham paid a world record transfer fee of £10,650 to obtain his services. His Oldham debut brought him a try in a 39-13 victory over Barrow on 21 March 1959. In his only full season, 1959/60, with Oldham he scored 31 tries but never really settled in Lancashire. His career at Watersheddings saw him pile up 54 tries in only 52 matches, including six in a Cup-tie against Walney Central.

He was transferred back to Workington Town who broke the world record again by buying him back for £11,002 10s, which was 50 shillings (£2.50) more than St Helens had recently paid to Wigan for Mick Sullivan. Ike continued to play for Workington Town until 1968, making his last appearance in a 25-9 home victory over Swinton on 5 October 1968. His career with Town encompassed 375 games, in which he amassed 1,432 points from 274 tries and 305 goals. His record of 274 tries for the club has never been beaten although, oddly enough, even Ike never managed to match Johnny Lawrenson's club record of 49 tries in a season set in 1951/52. His best tally was 45 tries in 1957/58 when he also kicked 79 goals for a total of 293 points, another personal best.

Ike Southward's true stature in the game can be gauged from his record at the very top level – representative and test match rugby. His career at this level began on 11 April 1956, when he replaced the suspended Billy Boston as Great Britain's right-winger in an 18-10 victory over France in a floodlit international at Odsal. Four days later he landed a couple of goals for English Services RL, who lost 18-10 to French Services in Marseilles. His club-mate Andy Key was in the English pack. Ike also represented the British Army at Twickenham in the inter-services Rugby Union tournament in March 1956. He scored both tries in a 6-3 win against the Navy and another in a 26-9 loss to the RAF.

Ike won eleven Great Britain test caps and was a British Lion on the tours of 1958 and 1962. He was a key member of the brilliant 1958 team which won the Ashes in Australia and had the rare distinction of scoring tries in all three tests. He also played in the second and third tests of 1959 against the Aussies when the Ashes were retained, scoring a crucial try in the deciding test at Wigan.

Perhaps the most revealing statistic as to Ike's standing in the game lies in the fact that he is one of only six players in the history of the game to score 300 tries and 300 goals. The other superstars who have achieved this feat are Jim Lomas (a fellow Cumbrian from Maryport), Jim Leytham, Eric Ashton, Neil Fox and Garry Schofield.

Ike's career took in 486 games and yielded 1,840 points from 376 tries and 356 goals. After finishing his career with Whitehaven in 1969, Ike subsequently coached both Whitehaven and Workington Town in the 1970s and was also once coach of Cumbria County.

Jack Stoddart
Prop, second-row

First-class debut
1 October 1932, Swinton v. St Helens (away)
Last game
28 April 1951, Swinton v. Halifax (away)
Cumberland debut
10 November 1937, v. Yorkshire at Hunslet
Cumberland caps
6, 1937-48
Club
Swinton

Swinton signed Jack Stoddart from Maryport for £50 on 24 June 1932. They certainly got a bargain as Jack, a vigorous, hard-tackling, strong scrummaging prop forward or second-rower, remained a Lion for nineteen years and made 367 first-team appearances.

Aged eighteen when he arrived at Swinton, it was obviously going to be some time before he would win a regular place in a pack which contained fellow Cumbrian giants Martin Hodgson, Miller Strong and Joe Wright and other top forwards such as Tommy Armitt, Fred Butters and Fred Beswick. In his first season Swinton were runners-up in the Championship to Salford and continued to test the best for a few years. In 1934/35 they won the Championship and, although he did not play in the final, Jack picked up a winner's medal, having played in eleven league fixtures.

He was a regular first-teamer by 1936/37, however, mostly packing down in the second-row with Hodgson. He scored his first try in his 54th game, ironically an abandoned fixture against Widnes on 5 December 1936. Jack did not often trouble the scorers, his final tally being a mere seventeen tries. He scored five tries in 1937/38, when Swinton agonisingly lost in the semi-finals of both the Challenge Cup, 0-6 to Salford, and the Championship, 2-5 to Leeds. He was joined at Swinton that season by his younger brother Fletcher, a half-back who scored a hat-trick on his debut.

In 1939/40 Swinton won the Lancashire League and the Lancashire Cup but Jack only played eight games during the season, including both legs of the Emergency Wartime League Championship final against Bradford, who beat Swinton 37-22 on aggregate. Between 1940 and 1945 he would play no Rugby League.

After the war, Jack became Swinton captain. He was thirty-one and arguably his best years had been lost. He had first been capped by Cumberland in 1937, when a 7-7 draw had been gained against Yorkshire, and he played in the only two other pre-war county games. He was still good enough to win another three Cumberland caps in the post-war period, but his representative career was effectively ruined by the war.

On 10 March 1947, Jack captained Swinton to a 7-2 victory over the French champions Carcassonne and scored the only try of the match. Six months later he led Swinton to an 8-6 win against the Kiwis. The 1947/48 season was Jack's testimonial year and 10,000 turned out in awful conditions for his benefit match, a scoreless draw against Salford, on New Year's Day 1948. His benefit realised £329, a lot of money in austere Britain. Jack played in all 41 of Swinton's fixtures.

Swinton reached the Championship semi-final in 1950 but lost heroically 9-0 at Huddersfield, Jack playing the full game despite a bad ankle injury. He retired the following year aged thirty-six.

First-class debut
3 February 1923,
Swinton v. Wakefield Trinity (home)
Last game
3 October 1934,
Swinton v. Salford (home) Lancashire Cup
Cumberland debut
29 September 1923,
v. Lancashire at Whitehaven
Cumberland caps
21, 1923-32
Club
Swinton

Miller Strong is a perfect name for a prop forward and Parton-born Miller Strong was a near perfect prop for the rules under which Rugby League was played in the inter-war period. He was reported to be 13st 10lb when he left Broughton Moor amateur Rugby League club in 1922 to play for Swinton. He eventually weighed well over 15st, which was exceptionally heavy in those days. An expert scrummager, he fulfilled all the duties expected of a prop in the donkey work of tackling and taking the ball forward.

In his first game for Swinton he was sent off. It would not be the only time, as scrummaging offences were often punished by dismissal. However, the fact that Miller played 348 games (12 tries, 1 goal) over eleven years for the Lions demonstrated his value to a team which developed into one of the most successful of the era.

His first three seasons brought near misses as Swinton gained momentum. He earned runners-up medals for the Lancashire Cup in 1923, when St Helens Recs beat Swinton 17-0 in the final, and for the Championship in 1925, when the Lions lost to Hull KR in the final. He did, however, collect a Lancashire League Championship medal in 1924/25, the first of four he would win.

The following season saw disappointment as Swinton lost in the final of the Lancashire Cup and were defeated in the Championship semi-final but there was ample compensation when Miller played in his first Challenge Cup final. Swinton beat Oldham 9-3 at Rochdale. In 1926/27 Miller played again in the Challenge Cup final, Oldham gaining revenge 26-7. A week earlier he had been in Swinton's victorious side in the Championship final at Warrington, where St Helens Recs were beaten 13-8.

Season 1927/28, however, eclipsed all his previous successes, as Swinton won All Four Cups with Miller playing in 46 games, including the final victories over Wigan (Lancashire Cup), Warrington (Challenge Cup) and Featherstone Rovers (Championship). Of course, nothing could better that but he was still to figure in losing Lancashire Cup and Challenge Cup finals in 1931/32 and in Championship final of 1932/33. Moreover, he won another Championship with Swinton in 1930/31.

Alongside seventeen winners and runners-up medals, Miller Strong could boast 21 Cumberland caps. He made his first appearances in 1923 in heavy defeats by Lancashire at Whitehaven and Yorkshire at Hunslet but was a mainstay for almost a decade. In 1927/28 and 1932/33 he enjoyed unbeaten seasons with Cumberland, adding two more winners' medals to his collection.

In the early years of his Swinton career Miller formed part of one of the strongest front rows in the game with Henry Blewer and Bert Morris. His later years were spent in an even better combination with test players Tommy Armitt and Joe Wright.

John Tembey
Centre, second-row, prop

First-class debut
14 January 1956, Whitehaven v. Leigh (away)
Last game
7 September 1968, Whitehaven v. Barrow
(home) Lancashire Cup
Cumberland debut
31 August 1959, v. Lancashire at
Workington
Cumberland caps
7, 1959-64
Test caps
2
Clubs
Whitehaven, St Helens

John Tembey began his career as a bustling centre and ended it as a ball-playing prop forward.

A product of Whitehaven Grammar School, he played amateur Rugby League for Kells before signing for Whitehaven. His debut in 1956 at Leigh saw him partnering Billy Garrett in the centre. At 6ft 1.5in and nudging 15st, John was a menacing figure in the back-line. In 1956/57 he struck up a fruitful left-wing partnership with the talented Syd Lowdon, as Whitehaven shocked the Rugby League world by reaching the Challenge Cup semi-final. Unfortunately for John, injury kept him out of the Odsal clash with Leeds, who went on to lift the Cup. It was as near as he would ever get to a Challenge Cup final.

Earlier that season he had shared a great triumph, scoring Whitehaven's first try in their historic 14-11 victory over the Kangaroos.

On 14 December 1957 he left his days in the centre behind him, when he appeared at second-row alongside Dick Huddart in a 24-19 home victory over Bradford Northern. His speed and mobility were perhaps just lacking to be a top class centre, but in the pack they were at times devastating.

By 1959 he had won county honours. His first season at that level brought him a County Championship winner's medal, as he figured in victories over Lancashire at Workington and Yorkshire at Hull, where he scored his only try for Cumberland.

After playing 145 games (44 tries, 26 goals)

for Whitehaven, he transferred to St Helens, making his debut on 6 January 1961 in a 30-6 home win against Barrow. He had renewed his awesome second-row partnership with Dick Huddart and with Saints he began to win the major honours denied him at Whitehaven. He played in victorious Lancashire Cup-winning sides in 1962, 1963 and 1964 and in the Western Division final triumph over Swinton in 1964. He also won a Lancashire League Championship medal in 1964/65 and a League Championship medal in 1965/66, having won a runners-up medal the previous season.

With Saints he moved through the pack to become a tremendous open-side prop, creating opportunities for some star-studded back divisions. The front row of John, Bob Dagnall and Cliff Watson was a rare combination of skill, nous and belligerence. His form was good enough to earn him a spot for the opening Ashes test of 1963 at Wembley and in Great Britain's clash with France at Perpignan in 1964, both of which unfortunately ended in defeats.

After playing in 137 games (20 tries) for Saints, John was out of the game for almost two years before returning to Whitehaven in 1967, playing another 22 games (3 tries). On 21 October 1967, he scored the only try of the game for 'Haven who defeated Saints 11-6.

Ted Thornburrow

Utility back, loose-forward

First-class debut
26 August 1922, Barrow v. Leigh (home)
Last game
20 January 1934,
Bradford Northern v. Hunslet (away)
Cumberland debut
28 October 1922, v. Yorkshire at Maryport
Cumberland caps
21, 1922-30
Clubs
Barrow, Bradford Northern

Ted, sometimes known as Eddie, Thornburrow was a native of Workington and became one of the most versatile players produced by Cumberland.

He joined Barrow in 1922, making his debut on the left wing in a 23-5 home defeat by Leigh but a week later, he was the match-winner with two tries in a 15-3 victory at Halifax. In his first season Barrow almost reached the Cup final, beating St Helens Recs 8-0, Keighley 5-0 and Oldham 12-0 and holding Leeds 0-0 in the semifinal at Broughton. Their luck ran out in the replay at Salford, however, Ted hardly having a chance on the wing as Leeds won 20-0.

Ted was again disappointed the following season, when he had moved to centre. Barrow reached the semis with Ted scoring a hat-trick in a 67-3 first round win against Dearham Wanderers, two tries in the second round against Hull KR and another in the third round against Warrington. Wigan hammered Barrow 30-5 at Salford in the semi amid accusations of rough play by the winners. Ted never did play in a final, losing in a third semi against Widnes in 1930, by which time he had become a looseforward. In 1925, as a scrum-half, he had experi-

enced defeat in the semi-final of the Lancashire Cup against Swinton.

Luck was certainly not on his side but Barrow were a pretty mediocre side in the decade Ted slogged his guts out for them. He played in every single back position and at loose-forward in his 306 appearances for the club in nine years, scoring 91 tries and a solitary goal – against Keighley in 1925.

He was deservedly granted a benefit match against Bramley, who were beaten 44-13 on 18 April 1931. This was also Barrow's last match on their old Little Park ground at Roose. One of Ted's last matches for Barrow, against Swinton, was the occasion of the opening of Craven Park on 29 August 1931, when a new record crowd of 16,167 attended.

Ted transferred to Bradford Northern shortly afterwards, making his debut in an 18-5 victory over Castleford on 7 November 1931. Although he had been transformed into a forward at Barrow, Bradford preferrred to use him at halfback and centre. He made 73 appearances for them, scoring sixteen tries.

Ted had a wonderful county career. After making his debut in 1922 he played 21 consecutive games for the county, appearing at wing, stand-off and scrum-half. In 1926/27 he scored tries in all three of Cumberland's games (v. Yorkshire, Lancashire and New Zealand) and the following season he gained a County Championship winner's medal. In 1929 he scored a crucial try in Cumberland's great 8-5 victory over the Australians at Workington, his only victory in five encounters against touring sides.

Ted's younger brother Jim played on the wing for Barrow in the 1938 Challenge Cup final.

Alec Troup
Second-row forward

First-class debut
16 April 1927, Barrow v. York (home)
Last game
13 April 1946, Barrow v. Dewsbury (away)
Cumberland debut
20 October 1928, v. Glamorgan &
Monmouthshire at Whitehaven
Cumberland caps
18, 1928-46
England caps
4
Test caps
2
Club
Barrow

Lancelot Alexander Troup was not born a Cumbrian but he certainly became one. He was born in Kirkwall in the Orkney Isles but moved to Maryport as a child. He played amateur Rugby League for Maryport and signed for Barrow in 1927, making his debut in the second-row in a 22-5 home win against York, alongside local icons such as Charlie Carr, Bill Burgess and Ted Thornburrow, a fellow Cumbrian.

Sandy-haired and sometimes with a moustache, Alec was one of the best second-rowers of the inter-war period, ideally built for the job at 5ft 11in and 14st. He was equally proficient in attack and defence, was a regular try-scorer and kicked goals when necessary. Moreover, he was an inspirational captain who led by example.

By 1928 he had won his first two county caps although it would be 1932 before he established himself as a permanent fixture in the Cumberland second-row. Together with Martin Hodgson and Paddy Dalton, the county had arguably its greatest ever back row in this period. Alec received County Championship winners' medals in 1932/33, 1933/34 and 1934/35 and was a try-scorer in a fabulous 17-16 success against the 1933 Kangaroos at Whitehaven.

At international level he also cut the mustard. He won a tour trial in 1932 but did not gain a place among the Lions. Undaunted, he played some of the best rugby of his career in the following years. He repre-

sented England against Australia at Gateshead in January 1934 and then played against France in Paris on 15 April 1934, in the first Anglo-French international. In 1935 and 1936 he played against Wales. A second tour trial followed and the 1936 selectors could not ignore him. He went with the Lions down under, played in fifteen tour fixtures, scored four tries and played in two tests in New Zealand.

In club rugby Alec had played in losing Challenge Cup semi-finals for Barrow in 1930 and 1935 and he never did appear in a trophy-winning team. The 1937/38 season under his captaincy almost changed all that. On 4 December 1937, Alec led Barrow to a superb 12-8 triumph over the Australians, just a few weeks after he became the first captain to take Barrow to a major final, when they lost to Warrington in the Lancashire Cup. The Challenge Cup brought even more excitement as Wembley was reached with Salford their opponents. It ended tragically, particularly for Alec, whose knee was severely injured early on. As the game entered its final minute the score was 4-4, when a limping Alec failed to collect a kick through and Albert Gear scored the winning try for Salford.

Alec retired at the start of the war but returned for the 1945/46 season, won a final Cumberland cap and ended a notable nineteen-year career, which extended well over 400 games.

First-class debut
24 October 1971,
Workington Town v. Huyton (away)
Last game
28 August 1983, Whitehaven v. Widnes (away)
Cumbria debut
24 October 1973, v. Australians at Whitehaven
Cumbria caps
19, 1973-82
England caps
1
Test caps
1
Clubs
Workington Town, Whitehaven

Mad as a hatter! Brave as a lion! It depended upon whose side Arnold 'Boxer' Walker was figuring. If he was in your team, he was the latter. If not, he was probably giving your team grief, one way or another.

Flaxen-haired, in his early professional career Arnie looked more like a choirboy than a tough guy. At 5ft 6in and ten stone odd, he was usually the smallest man on the pitch but his aggression, verbal and physical, seemed boundless. He appeared both fearless and reckless. In the end his career was ended by a broken neck sustained in a game against Widnes at Naughton Park.

As scrum-halves go, Boxer was one of the best. At one stage in his career *Open Rugby* magazine placed him at the top of their prestigious world ratings. Apart from his kamikaze bravery, he had all the attributes of a natural scrum-half – speed, intuition, good hands and the ability to gee up his team-mates.

He had been born in 1952 in Woodhouse, Whitehaven and he had played his junior Rugby League for Kells. However, it was Workington Town who signed him professionally in 1971. His first game saw him score the winning try at Huyton after substituting for Jacky Newall. He would win plenty more matches for Town over the next eight years, the club's last golden age.

In 1976, 1977, 1978 and 1979 Boxer played in four consecutive Lancashire Cup finals. Workington only won the 1977 final, when Boxer dropped two goals in a 16-13 triumph over Wigan. He won the man of the match award, and, uniquely, won it again in 1978 despite being on the losing side to Widnes. A prolific drop-goaler, he landed at least one in every round of the 1977 Lancashire Cup. His last game for Town was the Lancashire Cup final of 1979.

He then moved on to Whitehaven for a huge £30,000 fee, dropping another goal on his debut at Dewsbury on 20 January 1980. His first full season at Whitehaven, 1980/81, was sensational: 'Haven gained promotion to Division One, Arnie dropped 22 goals, more than anyone else in the league, he captained Cumbria to the County Championship and to a 9-3 victory over the New Zealanders at the Rec.

On 15 November 1980 he was drafted into the Great Britain team for the third test against New Zealand at Leeds. Typically he made more tackles than anyone else (28) as Britain levelled the series with a 10-2 win. A few months later he made his only other international appearance at the same venue, only to find himself in a horror story as England lost 1-5 to France.

His combined career record for the two Cumberland professional clubs amounted to 273 games, 64 tries, 44 goals, 70 drop goals and 350 points.

Syd Walmsley

Full-back, wing

First-class debut
21 February 1920, Millom v. Leeds (away)
Cup
Last game
16 April 1927,
Huddersfield v. Bradford Northern (home)
Cumberland debut
6 October 1920, v. Lancashire at St Helens
Cumberland caps
12, 1920-27
England caps
2
Clubs
Leeds, Huddersfield

The fact that Syd Walmsley was wounded in both legs while serving in the Coldstream Guards during the First World War did not stop him from winning high honours as a Rugby League player.

He first played Rugby Union for Westminster College before the war but joined Millom in 1920. His fourth game for the club was a first round Challenge Cup-tie at Leeds, who won 44-5. Syd scored a try in the first minute and Leeds had seen enough to know that they wanted him. A month later he made his debut as a Loiner in an 11-0 victory at Wakefield Trinity.

Initially he played as a winger but was also competent in the centre. Eventually, however, he became an outstanding full-back. In his first season at Headingley he top-scored with 100 points (16 tries, 26 goals) and in the following season, 1921/22, he equalled Charlie Haycox's club record by landing 67 goals. During that campaign he earned a Yorkshire Cup winner's medal, kicking a goal in the final at Halifax, where Dewsbury were defeated 11-3.

In 1923 Leeds drubbed Hull 28-3 in the Challenge Cup final before a crowd of 29,335 at Wakefield. In the 76th minute Syd became only the second full-back to score a try in a final, beginning and finishing a 75 yards movement. His all-round performance was as near to perfection as could be desired.

He played his 188th and last game for Leeds at Warrington on 13 April 1925, having amassed 35 tries and 167 goals. He then joined Huddersfield, for whom he played two seasons,

scoring 6 tries and 60 goals in 64 appearances. In 1925 he appeared in the Fartowners' 2-0 defeat by Dewsbury in the Yorkshire Cup final at Wakefield. In the 1926 final, installed as captain, he led them to a 10-3 victory over Wakefield at Headingley, converting both his side's tries. A few weeks later he landed three decisive goals in Huddersfield's 12-10 win against the New Zealanders.

Syd played regularly for Cumberland between 1920 and 1927, figuring at full-back and in all four three-quarter positions. His first seven appearances for the county ended in defeats before he tasted victory (20-0) against Yorkshire at Whitehaven in 1924. In 1925, at Fartown, he scored two tries and three goals in another notable (31-13) triumph over the Tykes, while the following year he was awarded the captaincy.

In 1923 Syd won an England cap in an 18-11 defeat of Wales at Fartown, converting two tries. A tour trial, as captain of the Reds, followed in 1924 and he was invited to tour Australasia but, as a teacher, he could not make the trip. He won a second England cap against Other Nationalities at Leeds on 15 October 1924. He was the only Cumbrian in the side on both his appearances for England.

First-class debut
10 April 1909, Leeds v. Oldham (home)
Last game
4 September 1926, York v. Hunslet (away)
Cumberland debut
25 October 1910, v. Yorkshire at Dewsbury
Cumberland caps
20, 1910-23
England caps
2
Test caps
1
Clubs
Leeds, York

Billy Ward, who played his amateur rugby for Whitehaven Recs and Egremont, was one of Cumberland's most famous exports to Yorkshire, where he played his entire professional career. That career lasted for seventeen years and established him as one of the most prolific scoring loose-forwards the game had produced in its first quarter-century.

Noted for his hard tackling style and for a fleetness of foot, which enabled him to perform in the backs on occasions, Billy Ward made his debut for Leeds in April 1909, just a month after his twentieth birthday. Little more than a year later he was a household name in the Northern Union.

His rise was meteoric. On 14 and 21 March 1910, he played in both the trial matches for selection for the first Lions tour of Australasia. On 9 April he won international recognition, when he played for England against Wales at Ebbw Vale. A week later he packed down for Leeds in their first Challenge Cup final, at Fartown against Hull. The game was drawn 7-7 and replayed two days later at the same venue. This time Leeds ran away with the game 26-12 and Billy's winner's medal was a fine going away present,

as he left England with the Lions a few days later.

Billy, listed at 5ft 10in and 13st 4lb in official tour statistics, had the privilege of playing in the first test match played by the Lions abroad on 18 June at Sydney, when Australia were beaten 27-20. His tour was, however, ruined by injury and he played just four matches in Australia and none in New Zealand.

On returning to England he soon won his first county cap, scoring a try on his debut against Yorkshire. With a certain symmetry his career for Cumberland ended with another try-scoring appearance against the Tykes in 1923. His only County Championship winner's medal was earned in 1911/12.

Billy's career at Headingley also continued until 1923, bringing him appearances in the Yorkshire Cup finals of 1919 (lost) and 1921 (won) and the Championship final of 1915 (lost). Leeds routed Hull 28-3 in the Challenge Cup final in 1923 but he did not play in any of the rounds.

Billy scored 84 tries for Leeds in 279 peacetime matches, plus another fifteen tries during the First World War. His tally of tries was well over the century when his representative matches and later career at York are added. That was a phenomenal scoring rate for a forward in Billy Ward's era and a testament to his skill and durability.

Inevitably he was a try-scorer on his debut for York in an 8-15 loss at Hunslet on 24 November 1923, going on to make 103 appearances for the club, scoring eighteen tries.

First-class debut
10 November 1900,
Cumberland v. Cheshire at Birkenhead
Last game
9 September 1911,
Salford v. Broughton Rangers (away)
Cumberland caps
11, 1900-10
England caps
1
Test caps
2
Clubs
Broughton Rangers, Salford

Silas Warwick is now a name unfamiliar to followers of Rugby League, even in his native Cumberland. Yet, as the first Cumbrian to win test honours, he really should be better remembered.

Silas came from Whitehaven and began his senior career with Whitehaven Recreation, from where he won his first county cap in 1900. He was signed by Broughton Rangers, the current Challenge Cup holders and Champions, in 1902, making his debut on 13 September in a 17-3 home win over Hull. In two seasons with the Rangers, Silas played 36 games without scoring, as Rangers continued to figure in the top rankings but failed to win any trophies.

In 1904 he moved to neighbouring Salford, first appearing for them on Christmas Eve in a 6-11 home defeat by Leigh. Silas was a dashing forward, good in the open and useful in the scrums, who stood 5ft 11in and weighed 13st 8lb in his prime. He had joined another good team but again he was unfortunate when it came to winning competitions. In 1906 he did play in a Challenge Cup final only for Bradford to defeat his team 5-0 at Headingley. Even worse, Silas and Bradford forward Harry Feather were sent off for fighting. He played for Salford in losing semi-finals in 1907 against Oldham and 1910 against Hull.

However, his representative career burgeoned at Salford. He regained his Cumberland place after six years in 1906, going on to win eleven caps. Included among them were historic victories over the New Zealanders (21-9) at Workington in 1907, when he was a try-scorer,

and in the brutal affair at Carlisle in 1909, when the Australians were beaten 11-2.

Test match Rugby League was inaugurated when the Northern Union met New Zealand at Headingley on 25 January 1908. Silas Warwick was part of that historic occasion, coming into the side when Runcorn forward Dick Padbury withdrew. The Northern Union triumphed 14-6 and Silas, the only Cumbrian on view, had a blinder, one critic describing him as 'brilliant at times'. He and Asa Robinson were the pick of the forwards, another critic praising 'the right hand forward from Salford' for creating Robinson's second try. Silas retained his position for the second test at Chelsea, but the New Zealanders levelled the series with an 18-6 victory.

A few months later, on Easter Monday, 20 April 1908, Silas appeared in the first England-Wales international match at Tonypandy but again finished on the losing side.

Three years later, Silas had finished with the game, having played his 208th and final game for Salford. He had scored twenty tries for the club and one solitary goal, in a first round 64-0 Challenge Cup rout of the amateurs York INL in 1910.

First-class debut
27 October 1945, Hull v. Batley (home)
Last game
8 September 1959,
Hull v. Bramley (away) Yorkshire Cup
Cumberland debut
26 September 1946,
v. Yorkshire at Workington
Cumberland caps
12, 1946-58
Club
Hull

Not many players score over 200 tries in first class Rugby League but Ivor Watts achieved that landmark, playing on the wing for Hull.

Ivor Watts was born in Wales but moved to Cumberland as a child and consequently won eligibilty to represent his adopted county. Workington AFC and Workington Town both sought the Glasson Rangers player's signature, but it was Hull who obtained his services in 1945. He made his debut in an 10-8 defeat by Batley at The Boulevard, scoring a try from the right wing. For the rest of the season he was employed in the centre, which was rather unusual considering his diminutive stature – 5ft 7in and around 12st.

Hull reached the Yorkshire Cup final in his second season, Ivor bagging two tries in both the second round against York and in a gripping semi-final victory over Hull KR. Wakefield Trinity beat his team 10-0 in the final at Headingley before a crowd of 29,000. It would be seven years before he would figure in another major final and by then he had abandoned the centre and was a permanent fixture on the left wing, thrilling crowds with his quick, elusive running and excellent finishing.

Cumberland got good service from Ivor. His debut in 1946 against Yorkshire at Borough Park, Workington ended in a 11-9 defeat and it was another six years before he won his second cap. Between 1953 and 1958, however, he was a regular in the side, adding another ten caps to his tally. Although Cumberland lost 18-27 to Yorkshire in 1957, Ivor had the satis-faction of scoring two tries before his home crowd at The Boulevard.

In the mid-1950s Hull began to contest strongly for honours. Ivor was on the wing in his second Yorkshire Cup final in 1953, only to receive a runners-up medal against Bradford Northern. Another runners-up medal issued from the final of 1955, when Halifax beat Hull. There were two Championship-winners' medals for him though in 1955/56, when he missed the final against Halifax, and in 1957/58 when Workington Town were beaten 20-3 at Odsal. He also played in the final of 1957, Hull losing to Oldham. In 1959 he appeared at Wembley opposite the immortal Billy Boston as Wigan crushed the Boulevarders 30-13. Hull got to the final again in 1960 but by then Ivor had played the last of his 410 games for Hull. He had still been good enough to score five tries in his 409th game, a 45-10 home victory over Dewsbury.

Ivor's total of 216 tries was a club record, beating the previous best of 166 by Welsh international winger Alf Francis. It would take another fabulous Welsh winger, Clive Sullivan, to wrest the record from little Ivor.

Bill Wedgwood
Winger, centre

First-class debut
6 September 1902, Halifax v. Hull KR (home)
Last game
23 March 1912, Halifax v. Hull (away) Cup
Cumberland debut
15 October 1904, v. Cheshire at Birkenhead
Cumberland caps
6, 1904-09
Club
Halifax

William Robson Wedgwood was playing on the wing for Seaton reserves when he was fifteen. His first centre was the great Billy Little, who was followed by Tom Fletcher. In the 1901/02 season Fletcher helped Wedgwood to create a Seaton club record by running in 29 tries.

In 1902 Halifax lured the eighteen-year-old Bill away from Cumberland but had to pay Seaton a transfer fee of £10! It was money well spent. Bill immediately settled down on the Halifax wing with some storming displays. He was fast, possessed a disconcerting swerve and, at 6ft and over 13st, he was exceptionally strong for an Edwardian wingman. He was also an excellent goal-kicker, although his talents in that direction were usually superfluous at Halifax because of the presence of Billy Little.

His first season at Thrum Hall was stunningly successful. Although Bill missed fourteen straight games when injured at Runcorn on 8 November 1902, he was back in time for the Challenge Cup-ties. He scored points in ties against Salterhebble, Castleford, Brighouse Rangers and Hull, only failing to score in the final itself against Salford, which Halifax won 7-0 at Headingley before a record crowd of 32,509. The following week, however, he played the game of his life. Halifax had to win their last fixture, at Leigh, to lift the Championship. They won 11-0 to achieve the double with Bill the toast of Halifax, having scored all the points – three tries and a goal.

The following season Halifax retained the Challenge Cup, beating Warrington 8-3 at Salford. Bill received a second winner's medal but unaccountably was left out of the final.

There were more medals for him in later years. In 1905 he played in the first Yorkshire Cup final but had to settle for a runners-up medal, as Halifax went down to Hunslet. There was a second Championship medal for him in 1906/07, when he played in fifteen league fixtures and scored in every one of them. In 1908/09 there was another pair of winners' medals as Halifax lifted both the Yorkshire Cup and Yorkshire League.

Much of Bill's later career was played as a centre and it was from there that he scored a personal best 20 points (7 goals, 2 tries) against Wakefield on 8 December 1906. His winger Percy Eccles scored five tries. Bill's Halifax service amounted to 150 games, 47 tries and 120 goals.

Bill, a gunsmith by profession, put in some notable performances for Cumberland, both as a centre and winger. He effectively won the clash with Lancashire at Whitehaven in 1905, scoring eight points in an 11-0 victory. In his last game against the Australians at Carlisle in 1909, he was a try-scorer in a famous 11-2 triumph.

First-class debut
2 September 1899, *v.* Leigh (home)
Last game
13 March 1920, *v.* Halifax (home)
Cumberland debut
7 October 1905, *v.* Lancashire at Wigan
Cumberland caps
16, 1905-19
Club
Broughton Rangers

Penrith has rarely been a prolific breeding ground for Rugby League players but in Billy Winskill it produced a gem for the Northern Union. Billy was born in 1877 and began playing for Penrith Juniors when he was fifteen, moving on to the United Club a couple of years later. At eighteen he played for Percy Park in Northumberland for a year before returning to the United Club. He finally left Penrith for Lancashire, when he signed for Broughton Rangers in August 1899. He would serve their pack, and occasionally their three-quarters, loyally and well for almost 21 years.

A critic wrote of him, 'A spirited player with sound judgement when sound defensive tactics are necessary, makes him a valuable asset. He has all the natural tenacity of a Cumbrian. Not a showy player but is all there in the pack and if a rush is necessary he is daring and may be relied upon to take the risk.'

Broughton Rangers were one of the very best teams in the Northern Union when Winskill was signed. He quickly made his mark, being selected to play for the Rest against the Champions (Runcorn) at the end of his first season. In 1901/02 Rangers became the first club to achieve the league and cup double. Billy played in 20 of their 26 Championship games, as Broughton left everyone in their wake, runners-up Salford finishing twelve points adrift. On 26 April 1902 Rangers murdered Salford 25-0 in the Challenge Cup final at Rochdale, Billy being well to the fore.

Surprisingly, it was not until 1905 that Billy was capped by Cumberland in a 3-3 draw against Lancashire. This began a county career which remarkably lasted for fourteen years and ended when he was forty-two. Included were games against the New Zealanders in 1908 – a famous victory at Workington – and a narrow defeat against the Australians at Maryport in 1911.

Although Broughton Rangers had declined as a major force, they surprised everyone by reaching the Challenge Cup final in 1911. Their opponents at Salford were hot favourites Wigan. Billy and his pack, half of whom were Cumbrians, strangled the life out of Wigan, however, in pouring rain on a mudbound pitch and won 4-0. At 14st 10lb, Billy was the heaviest man on the pitch. The Earl of Derby presented him with his winner's medal.

During the First World War, Billy took up soccer as an inside forward and won a bronze medal in the Army Camp Championship at Oswestry. He returned to play a dozen games for Broughton in the 1919/20 season, finishing his career as a Ranger with 349 appearances.

In later life he became landlord of The Vine Inn, near to Broughton Rangers' ground. His son, William, played soccer for Accrington Stanley.

Ian Wright
Centre

First-class debut
17 September 1966,
Workington Town v. Salford (home)
Last game
13 May 1979,
Workington Town v. Castleford (home)
Cumberland debut
11 September 1968, v. Yorkshire at Whitehaven
Cumberland caps
9, 1968-74
Club
Workington Town

The newspapers said it cost Workington Town £1,500 to gain Ian Wright's signature in August 1966. He was worth it, even though it was a lot to pay for a teenage Rugby Union stand-off in those days. Ian played for Cockermouth RU but lived near Brian Edgar in Broughton.

Although he was a stand-off for Cockermouth, he only played once for Town at number six. Apart from another half-dozen games on the wing, all his 302 games were played in the centre, where his speed, strength and eye for the opening made him one of the best of his generation.

His first appearance at Derwent Park gave an indication of what would follow when he scored a hat-trick for the reserves against Rochdale Hornets 'A'. Ian certainly had try-scoring instincts and his total of 168 for Town is bettered only by Ike Southward. His first try for Town came in his second appearance at Wigan on 24 September 1966 and at the end of his debut season he topped the club lists with eighteen. He went on to be Town's leading try-scorer in eight seasons, the last six consecutively. But for injuries which kept him out for almost the entire 1967/68 season and for the whole of 1971/72, Ian would certainly have broken the 200 try barrier.

Coming back from injury in 1968/69, he had his most prolific campaign, scoring 23 tries. The only centre to score more was Leeds's Syd Hynes. Ian made his debut for Cumberland during the season and won selection for England Under 24s. He scored two tries in a 42-2 victory over France at Castleford, while Town winger Keith Davies claimed three. Ian twice scored four tries for Town against Swinton and Blackpool, a feat he would repeat six seasons later against Doncaster.

Workington never came near to winning anything in Ian's time until 1975/76, when they gained promotion but lost for the third consecutive season in the Lancashire Cup semi-finals. They then reached the Lancashire Cup final in his last three seasons. In 1976 Ian scored in all the rounds except the final, when Widnes beat Town. In 1977 he scored the opening try, a beauty off Les Gorley, in the final against Wigan, Town winning 16-13. In 1978 he settled for another runners-up medal, Widnes again winning.

Even in his last season Ian topped Town's try-scorers with thirteen, including a hat-trick in a glorious 31-11 triumph at Leeds. It was odd, then, that his career for Cumberland brought him just one try and he had to wait until his last game, a 19-12 win against Other Nationalities at Whitehaven in 1974, to claim it. Ian's county career began with seven defeats in a row and he did not taste victory for six years until Yorkshire were beaten 10-7 at Workington, two weeks before he scored that solitary try.

Joe Wright
Prop-forward

First-class debut
3 November 1928, Swinton v. Halifax (home)
Last game
17 November 1945,
Swinton v. Workington Town (away)
Cumberland debut
20 September 1930, v. Yorkshire at Whitehaven
Cumberland caps
19, 1930-38
England caps
3
Test caps
1
Club
Swinton

Joe Wright was born in Carlisle and played Rugby Union for the local club before joining Swinton. Swinton had just written their name large in the annals of the game by winning everything in 1927/28, becoming the third and last club to win All Four Cups. Joe Wright forced his way into that superb side in November 1928 and hardly missed a game for the next twelve years.

Joe was a prop, who stood 5ft 9in and weighed 14st. He was a rare handful in the scrums, a powerful tackler and a man who would last the full 80 minutes. He and fellow Cumbrian Miller Strong, a bigger but less mobile man than Joe, were as potent a pair of props as Swinton or Cumberland could have hoped for.

Swinton won the Lancashire League Championship in Joe's first season and repeated the trick in 1930/31. It was not until 18 April 1931, that Joe scored his first points for the club, when he bagged four goals and a try in a 37-0 rout of Bradford Northern. In over 400 games for the Lions he would claim only thirteen tries but props were not expected to score tries. 1930/31 also brought him a Championship winner's medal as Swinton downed Leeds 14-7 in the final at Wigan.

The following season brought two agonising defeats for Swinton and runners-up

medals for Joe. In the Lancashire Cup final a last minute penalty gave Salford a 10-8 victory and in the Challenge Cup final Swinton lost 11-8 to Leeds. It was not all bad news for Joe, however, for on 27 January 1932 he was capped by England, who beat Wales 19-2 at Salford. He then played in two of the three tour trials and was selected in the Lions party for Australasia. On tour he played in sixteen fixtures and scored three tries, making his only test appearance at Auckland in the final game against New Zealand, which was won 20-18.

He made further appearances for England in victories over Other Nationalities at Workington in 1933 and France in Paris in 1934, the first Anglo-French international. His Cumberland career brought him 19 caps and three consecutive County Championship medals for 1932/33, 1933/34 and 1934/35, when he was an ever-present. He also played in Cumberland's victory over the 1933 Kangaroos. Remarkably he had played in three Swinton teams which defeated the Australians in 1929, 1933 and 1937.

More domestic medals were added to his tally – a Championship winners in 1934/35, and a runners-up in 1932/33, while in 1939/40 Swinton took the Lancashire Cup and finished runners-up in the Emergency League Championship – Joe's last games for five years. He returned briefly after the war and, fittingly, his last game saw him score the only try in Swinton's 3-2 victory at Workington.

Harold Young
Loose-forward

First-class debut
4 September 1926, Bradford Northern v.
Wakefield Trinity (away)
Last game
16 March 1935,
Bradford Northern v. Hunslet (away)
Cumberland debut
8 January 1927,
v. New Zealanders at Workington
Cumberland caps
16, 1927-32
England caps
4
Tests caps
1
Clubs
Bradford Northern, Huddersfield, Castleford

Harold Young, a native of Kells, played amateur rugby with Kells and Hensingham. He came from a notable sporting family. His elder brother Joe was an inside forward for Accrington Stanley and Spurs, who also boxed well enough to have survived five rounds against the legendary fly-weight champion Jimmy Wilde. Harold's younger brother Victor, who played for Hull KR and Hunslet, won three Cumberland County caps as a winger in 1936 and 1937.

Most unusually, Harold did not become a professional Rugby League player until he was twenty-six years old. Having been a miner at Ladysmith Pit, he accepted Bradford Northern's offer of a first-team place and a job in a Bradford mill in 1926. In only his seventh game he was thrown in against the New Zealand tourists, who despatched Northern 38-17. Northern finished next to bottom of the League, having won only six games all season but in Harold Young they had discovered a shining star.

Harold finished his first season as Bradford's leading try-scorer with eight touchdowns and won the first of sixteen Cumberland caps against the New Zealanders at Workington's Lonsdale Park. For the next half-dozen years Harold was an automatic choice at loose-forward for the county, helping Cumberland to the Championship in 1927/28 and 1932/33. In 1929 he figured in one of the county's greatest ever triumphs when the Australians were defeated 8-5 at Workington.

Harold was noted for his wonderful tackling and attributed his skill in that sphere to his Cumberland and Westmoreland wrestling background. One of his specialities was the hip tackle and his prority was always to land on top of his victim. For a Rugby League forward Harold was not a big man – 5ft 11in and barely 13st in his prime – but he was tee-total, fit and full of energy. His side-stepping, apparently, was wonderful for a forward.

Open-faced and prematurely bald, Harold was certainly getting noticed at Bradford. Such was his form that he was selected for a tour trial at Headingley (1 February 1928). His opponent was the redoubtable Frank Gallagher, one of League's all-time great loose-forwards. The conditions were vile, so bad in fact that one winger was taken from the field suffering from exposure. It did not seem to bother Harold, who played a blinder. His performance clinched his place on the 1928 Lions tour to Australia and New Zealand, becoming Bradford Northern's first tourist.

Harold played nine games on tour and scored six tries, including a hat-trick against Bundaberg. The 1928 Lions had the novel experience of playing two exhibition games in Canada at Montreal and Vancouver. The games were billed as England v. Wales and, because of a slight shortfall in Welshmen, Harold played for Wales on both occasions!

third important clash, the Yorkshire Cup final, at Halifax between Huddersfield and Leeds. There was only a runners-up medal on this occasion, however, as Leeds won 10-2. The following season did provide Harold with a Yorkshire Cup-winners' medal as Huddersfield won the 1931 final 4-2 against Hunslet. Harold could not play in the final but had played in the first two rounds to earn his medal. That season saw Harold appear in his third Championship final with Huddersfield but St Helens defeated them 9-5 at Wakefield.

Harold Young played his 121st and final game (17 tries) for Huddersfield at Wakefield Trinity on 14 April 1933. Truth to tell, he was glad to leave. Despite the club's success, many players contemporary with Harold shared his distrust of the Fartown management. Harold's own description of the men who ran Fartown was 'uppity'. The team played wonderful, enter-prising, open rugby and did not mess about with unnecessary heavy forward play which suited Harold well enough. The off-field scene was not so harmonious.

Fartown had, however, put Harold on a big stage. In 1929/30 there was a Kangaroo tour to England and an amazing Ashes series had ended all square for the only time in history following a scoreless draw in the third test at Swinton. When the team was selected to play a unique fourth test at Rochdale on 15 January 1930, Harold was awarded his first and only test cap. He was a month short of his thirtieth birthday. The game, as tight as can be imagined, ended in a 3-0 victory for Great Britain and Harold had played a part in a historic League occasion.

On leaving Huddersfield, Harold briefly played for Castleford making seven appearances for them including a 6-39 defeat by the Kangaroos. By Christmas Day 1933, the wheel had turned full circle and Harold was once more packing down at the back of Bradford Northern's scrum as Bramley were beaten 8-6 at the old Birch Lane ground. He played on into the next season (1934/35), despite a recurring leg injury which precipitated his retirement. It was a momentous season for Northern who moved from Birch Lane to Odsal Stadium. His second spell with Northern comprised 25 games (two tries). His first-class career covered exactly 250 games (39 tries) despite his late, late start.

Oddly enough, Harold had made his official international debut for England against Wales at Wigan on 11 January 1928 in a 20-12 victory and went on to win four England caps, two against the Welsh and two against Other Nationalities. On each occasion Harold finished on the winning side.

On his return from the tour impecunious Bradford Northern bowed to the inevitable and let Harold transfer to aristocratic Huddersfield in exchange for Fartown half-backs Reed and Jones. Harold's last game for Northern came in a 3-35 loss at Dewsbury on 27 October 1928. He had made 65 appearances and bagged ten tries.

Huddersfield were a major power in the game and Harold was to enjoy a good deal of success at Fartown. By the end of his first season he had earned a Yorkshire League Championship winners' medal and had played in Huddersfield's Rugby League Championship-winning final XIII in a tense 2-0 victory over Leeds at Halifax. Huddersfield repeated the same double in 1929/30 and the Championship final was even closer as Huddersfield and Leeds drew 2-2 at Wakefield. Harold and his mates retained the trophy, however, with a 10-0 triumph in the replay at Halifax. The 1930/31 season saw a